T0120789

The Art of Reciting Scripture

*To speak the Word clearly and naturally with
an understanding that animates the passage*

Thomas L. Griffin

WESTBOW
P R E S S®
A DIVISION OF THOMAS NELSON
& ZONDERVAN

Copyright © 2020 Thomas L. Griffin.

All rights reserved. No part of this book may be used or reproduced by
any means, graphic, electronic, or mechanical, including photocopying,
recording, taping or by any information storage retrieval system
without the written permission of the author except in the case of
brief quotations embodied in critical articles and reviews.

This book is a work of non-fiction. Unless otherwise noted, the author
and the publisher make no explicit guarantees as to the accuracy of
the information contained in this book and in some cases, names of
people and places have been altered to protect their privacy.

WestBow Press books may be ordered through booksellers or by contacting:

WestBow Press
A Division of Thomas Nelson & Zondervan
1663 Liberty Drive
Bloomington, IN 47403
www.westbowpress.com
844-714-3454

Because of the dynamic nature of the Internet, any web addresses or
links contained in this book may have changed since publication and
may no longer be valid. The views expressed in this work are solely those
of the author and do not necessarily reflect the views of the publisher,
and the publisher hereby disclaims any responsibility for them.

Any people depicted in stock imagery provided by Getty Images are
models, and such images are being used for illustrative purposes only.
Certain stock imagery © Getty Images.

ISBN: 978-1-6642-0796-7 (sc)
ISBN: 978-1-6642-0795-0 (hc)
ISBN: 978-1-6642-0794-3 (e)

Library of Congress Control Number: 2020919264

Print information available on the last page.

WestBow Press rev. date: 12/17/2020

Scripture quotations marked (NIV) are taken from the Holy Bible, New International Version®, NIV®. Copyright © 1973, 1978, 1984, 2011 by Biblica, Inc.® Used by permission of Zondervan. All rights reserved worldwide. www. zondervan.com The "NIV" and "New International Version" are trademarks registered in the United States Patent and Trademark Office by Biblica, Inc.®

Scripture quotations marked (ESV) are from the ESV® Bible (The Holy Bible, English Standard Version®), copyright © 2001 by Crossway, a publishing ministry of Good News Publishers. Used by permission. All rights reserved.

Scripture marked (BBE) taken from the Bible in Basic English.

Scripture quotations marked (NLT) are taken from the Holy Bible, New Living Translation, copyright ©1996, 2004, 2015 by Tyndale House Foundation. Used by permission of Tyndale House Publishers, a Division of Tyndale House Ministries, Carol Stream, Illinois 60188. All rights reserved.

Quotes

"Recitation is about God being at work in the reciter, changing me and preparing me to be a vessel to carry His word out to others."
Charity Jacobs

"I put myself in the speaker's voice and feel the force of the words, from the exhortation of Moses in Deuteronomy 30 to the vitriol of the crowds in Luke 23 to the boldness of Stephen in Acts 7."
Colin Earle

"Practicing the memorization discipline is a barometer of my spiritual health. Reviewing a passage over and over reveals meaning one might not have discovered."
Tim Porter

"The most lasting three minutes I have ever prepared for. Recite on stage once and the Word dwells in you for life."
Ryan Awori

"Preparing for my recitation helped me to picture the events quite vividly, like the cliché 'it made it come alive'—but that's true! A great learning experience!"
Kerry Wheatcroft

To my little family: Carol, Anne, and Rebecca

Contents

Foreword

You who bring good news to Zion, go up on a high
mountain. You who bring good news Jerusalem,
lift up your voice with a shout, lift it up, do not be
afraid.

Isaiah 40:9 NIV

The Art of Reciting Scripture is a breath of fresh air for the church of
Christ. I believe in what Tom Griffin has written for personal reasons.
My Christian life has been deeply shaped through memorizing and
reciting Scripture. As a young child, Scripture memory was a regular
part of our family-of-ten dinner routine. My dad would have us
practice reciting "The Roman Road"—Romans 3:10, 3:23, 5:8, 6:23,
and 10:10–13—and many other portions of Scripture like Psalm
23, John 3:16, and Ephesians 2:8–9. I remember church Bible drill
competitions, which sometimes included quoting verses of the Bible.

As a young adult, I was blessed to have a Bible teacher with a
passion for memorizing Scripture. Jerry challenged us to memorize
and recite chapters of the Bible—Psalms 1, Romans 8, 1 Corinthians
13, and others. He even challenged us to recite books of the Bible,
such as 1 Peter and 1 John.

As a pastor and preacher, I've found it helpful to memorize the
passages that I preach because it helps both me and the hearers
imagine the message as being delivered by the original speaker.
Memorizing a text also helps to eliminate the extremely annoying

habit of us preachers mispronouncing difficult names and places or stumbling through the passage while reading, because recitation requires that you read the text many times and rehearse the words of the text, realizing that they're divinely inspired and worthy of correct pronunciation and delivery. This blessing, of course, isn't only for preachers but also for any disciple who wants to understand and communicate God's Word to others. I'm a firm believer in memorizing and reciting Scripture. I see its benefits both to the reciter and the audience.

I welcome Tom's excellent and practical treatment of Bible recitation for Christian worship. I'm honored to recommend the book. Tom rightly treats recitation as a discipleship opportunity. It's a great way to pass on the practice of the apostle Paul, "The things you have heard me say in the presence of many witnesses entrust to reliable men who will also be qualified to teach others." (2 Timothy 2:2 NIV) I found the chapter on "Recitation Discipleship" to be especially practical. Tom describes a process of making disciples through recitation groups in four simple, understandable steps: trust building, learning, syntheses, and discipling others.

We learn by hearing, then doing, and then teaching others to do. Shortly after moving to Germany and getting involved in our church, Tom recited. His recitation was well received. He did it again and again and again. Our church has been blessed as Tom has recited and then encouraged and trained others to recite.

Tom is passionate about the practice of recitation. His life was changed as a result of getting involved in a ministry of recitation years ago. He's also passionate about training others to grow in Christ through memorizing and reciting Scripture. Tom's enthusiasm is contagious because he really believes that everyone will benefit from recitation. His ministry has brought a fresh spirit of joy and appreciation of God's Word in our fellowship of believers. I've been encouraged and challenged to hear people in our local congregation recite God's Word in a way that captures the heart and mind and stirs the imagination. Seated on the front row, Tom is often the one who is "on book" (see chapter 4 for an explanation) to help if needed. Everyone in the congregation is listening intently to the reciter because we are "for them" and "with them," knowing that God's written word is being spoken.

The Art of Reciting Scripture will enable anyone interested in growing as a follower of Jesus through Scripture memory and recitation to have a practical tool. The book will be even more valuable if someone—anyone—will take the material to develop a discipleship ministry of recitation in his or her church or group. They'll be blessed and will be a blessing to many others.

I'm eager to see this tool of discipleship made available to God's church. I recommend it to pastors and other leaders and to all followers of Jesus who want to grow as disciples or who may be searching for a ministry in the church. The prophet Isaiah spoke of the enduring quality of God's Word: "The grass withers and the flowers fall, but the word of our God endures forever" (Isaiah 40:8 NIV). Investing in what is eternal brings blessings now and forever.

Jimmy Martin
General Secretary, International Baptist Convention
Elder, International Christian Fellowship Oberursel, Germany

Introduction

From the outrageous to the sublime, from technical facts to juicy gossip, we're bombarded daily with more information than we can handle. It piles up like cars on a slippery highway. We've come so far in terms of broadcasting words out to others, yet we struggle to know the Word inside ourselves, to have it written on our hearts (Psalm 40:8 NIV). In this age of bountiful information, there's a famine of not only hearing the words of the Lord (Amos 8:11–12 NIV) but also of understanding their depth. They remain outside of us, competing for our thoughts on the open market.

The message of Christ is meant to be written so deep into us (2 Corinthians 3:3 NIV) that it flows out of our pores and speaks to our children (Deuteronomy 6:7 NIV). We are meant to be adorned with the Word (Deuteronomy 6:8 NIV) so that it flows naturally in our conversations and actions so that we are continually reminded of both its overwhelming benefits and the cost of disobedience. How can we come close to *being* the message when we aren't familiar with the words themselves?

This book describes one method by which we can elevate the Word above the cacophony around us and meld it into our lives. There's nothing new about the idea of memorizing Scripture, but the thought of reciting those same words to an audience seems to take us unawares. This book seeks to address that gap by exploring the nuance, variety, and range of techniques involved in reciting Scripture.

1

Reciting Scripture Explained

Fix these words of mine in your hearts and minds;
tie them as symbols on your hands and bind them
on your foreheads. Teach them to your children,
talking about them when you sit at home and when
you walk along the road, when you lie down and
when you get up. Write them on the doorframes of
your houses and on your gates.

Deuteronomy 11:18–21 NIV

Do you take those words seriously? I ask because you don't seem to
have anything attached to your forearms or bound to your foreheads.
If anyone were to visit your house, would he or she find writings on
your door frames? Let me ask a different question then. What's your
understanding of the following passage?

For we are the aroma of Christ to God among
those who are being saved and among those who
are perishing.

2 Corinthians 2:15 ESV

Does it mean that you are meant to be scented like one of
those candles down at the mall? If taken literally, you should be

pungent, covered with stick-it notes, and have a house with walls covered in writing. I think that you'll agree, however, that there's a bigger message here, a message about how the word of God should permeate your life, and how you should project that into the world.

Read the 2 Corinthians passage just a bit further. Verse 16 (NIV) describes believers as having the potential to be "an aroma that brings life." What an incredible opportunity! Not to be an oddity with placards stuck to you and covered with perfume but to be so invested in the Word of God that it shapes you in a way that attracts others to the giver of life.

This is the context that lands us at the door of recitation and aligns our intent with our call to action. The fundamental activities are memorizing Scripture and speaking it to anyone who will listen, not as a performance meant to impress but as a gift meant to bring life to those around us. We strive to speak it and live it in a natural way that encourages believers, captivates the lost, and honors our Savior.

The recitation ministry is an extension of the spiritual discipline of Scripture memory. Reciting means that you will learn a Biblical passage intimately and then share it by speaking it aloud, from memory. It's a challenging process of discipleship that's meant to develop you personally as well as to provide a witness that influences those around you.

As you progress through the process, you'll also learn the patterns that will help you to disciple others within your church family, to inspire your family at home, and to spread the message to your community.

Reciters decide on a passage, either one self-selected or one that is proposed by someone else, and then memorize it. Maybe you've already decided on a passage. If not, check chapter 5 in this book for tips on how to choose a passage. Once you decide on a passage, you'll spend time studying and memorizing the passage (refer to chapter 6 for memorization techniques). As you do so, if you're diligent, you'll discover your voice to present the message as it was originally intended. It's only at this point that you'll earnestly turn your attention to how you'll animate the passage.

Recitation resembles acting, but it isn't. Whereas an actor endeavors to portray someone that he or she is not, a reciter is presenting someone they are striving to become. Acting is comparatively easy, since it's so creative. Recitation must stay true to both the intent of the passage as well as to the character of the reciter. I've found that reciters have their biggest challenge in just being themselves when reciting—not imitating an orator or injecting flair, but by being disciplined and staying true to their own character as he or she delivers the message of Scripture.

During rehearsals, you'll have a chance to examine the nuances that are unique to the passage, including tone and phrasing, that resolve it into a natural, animated communication. The goal is for you to speak the passage naturally—not like an actor or an orator but like yourself, as you would talk to your friends.

As you begin your recitation journey, understand that your purpose is as much about the development of others as it is about you. Recitation fits within the discipleship model, which means that as you grow, then you'll also help others to follow in your path.

2

Recitation Ministry Begins

It was a cool, overcast day, and he was reading from Acts chapter 5:33–36, the passage known as "Gamaliel's advice."

> When they heard this, they were furious and wanted to put them to death. But a Pharisee named Gamaliel, a teacher of the law, who was honored by all the people, stood up in the Sanhedrin and ordered that the men be put outside for a little while. Then he addressed the Sanhedrin: "Men of Israel, consider carefully what you intend to do to these men."
>
> Acts 5:33–35 NIV

The words of the story came slowly and with an even, passive tone. There were mistakes in pronunciation, awkward points of emphasis, and a stunning lack of appreciation for the gravity of the words being spoken.

Let's just say that it was uninspiring. It wasn't an isolated instance. We've all seen it before, someone trying to read a passage from a book, any book, with which he or she isn't familiar. They address the passage as if approaching an alien, and it isn't surprising that their words sound foreign.

But isn't reading the Bible a little more important than reading from the latest romance novel at the Saturday afternoon book club? Shouldn't there be a greater expectation on the person speaking these words?

The man continued the reading.

> Then he addressed the Sanhedrin: "Men of Israel, consider carefully what you intend to do to these men." (Acts 5:35 NIV)

What an extraordinary moment this was! Both dangerous and prophetic. A riveting, sage, tense moment, and yet the whole thing just seemed so half-hearted and mundane.

Sure, the reader meant well, but I thought that it would have been better had he not been reading it cold. Maybe if he'd read it aloud a few times to get familiar with the phrasing and researched the correct pronunciations and understood the context. Wouldn't it have been great if he had just told us the passage, looking directly at us, letting us breathe in the words and experience that moment, that moment which had been decades in the making, steeped in the martyrs and missteps of generations of the Jewish people? Wouldn't it have been something, I mean, really something, if that man, that well-meaning man, had *memorized* those words and then brought the grit and weight of that passage to life?

The day that this well-meaning man stumbled through Gamaliel's advice was the first day that I volunteered to be one of the lay readers of Scripture. However, I had a secret agenda. The decision was planted in my heart not only to familiarize myself with the passage in advance but also to actually memorize it and then speak it clearly and confidently. I'd love to tell you about the decision-making process or maybe about a heavenly host announcing my sacred mission, but the decision didn't even seem like a decision. It was just obvious what needed to be done. The whole thing was formed before the first inkling of it came to mind.

The passage assigned to me was from Acts 8:26–34. The story of Philip and the Ethiopian eunuch. It would take place in four weeks. Our daughter, Anne, had come into the world just a month before, and she often needed attention in the middle of the night, so I would pace the floor of our apartment, carrying Annie like a football and practicing the passage. "Have you heard the story of Philip and the Ethiopian eunuch?" I would ask her. Then I would proceed to stumble through reciting the story to my bundled-up captive audience.

> On his way he met an Ethiopian eunuch, an important official in charge of all the treasury of the Kandake (which means "queen of the Ethiopians").
>
> Acts 8:27 NIV

At two months old, Annie seemed to appreciate the note that there was a female leading the Ethiopians. She leaned into the story when Philip ran up to the chariot, and she paused when Philip asked, "Do you understand what you are reading?" (Acts 8:30 NIV)

Then came her favorite part, and she waited in expectant anticipation of the response (I may have read a little into her response).

> "How can I," he said, "unless someone explains it to me?" So he invited Philip to come up and sit with him.
>
> Acts 8:31 NIV

Philip quoted from Isaiah 53. I would fold Anne a little closer as the story reached its heart-warming conclusion.

> The eunuch asked Philip, "Tell me, please, who is the prophet talking about, himself or someone else?" Then Philip began with that very passage of Scripture and told him the good news about Jesus.
>
> Acts 8:34–35 NIV

It was a fitting passage to begin a ministry about understanding Scripture. All the elements were there: an eager audience; a person who had prepared for the moment; and a meeting between the two. This passage about understanding Scripture and calling for action would be the basis for a ministry about Scripture.

What had started as a simple act of obedience by Philip to "go to that chariot and stay near it" (Acts 8:29 NIV) turned into the conversion of a high official becoming a follower of the Lord. Sleeping Anne seemed to smile each time she heard the conclusion "and told him the good news about Jesus" (Acts 8:35 NIV).

Day by day I was able to make progress towards understanding and internalizing the passage.

Saint Philip Baptising the Ethiopian Eunuch by Aelbert Cuyp, photo credit: National Trust, Anglesey Abbey

As I prepared, I remembered the words of a friend, Jim, from the drama team at Valley Bible Church (VBC). First, some background.

The drama team at VBC would prepare and present short (four-to-seven minute) dramatic presentations during Sunday services that were intended to support the teaching for the day. The dramas could be humorous or satirical, but, more frequently, they were poignant and tense. Jim was the stalwart of the drama team, a trained actor and member of Actors' Equity (the stage actors' guild). He was our best actor, but after years of participating, he withdrew. Although he enjoyed acting, he had come to the conclusion that he was tired of memorizing words that he would just want to forget as soon as the presentation was over. He would rather memorize something that was *worth* memorizing, something of value. Something like the Bible. Jim's perspective was a turning point for me. I knew he was right.

The Sunday arrived for me to read the passage about Philip and the Ethiopian eunuch. I had the beginnings of carpal tunnel syndrome from hours of carrying Annie in the "football hold" and telling her the story. My heart was beating a little more quickly than the typical Sunday Scripture reader because my goal was not to read, but to recite. It was not only that I had never done this before, but also that I had never even *seen it* done before. When the time came, I walked to the front, stood behind the podium, and announced the Scripture for the day. Then, I took one step to the side of the podium and began, "Now an angel of the Lord said to Philip, 'Go'" (Acts 8:26 NIV).

I had experience in front of audiences. Thirteen years of teaching high school physics and ten years of drama ministry had prepared me to have some comfort with being in front of an audience. But this was different, and the doubts stood in line at the back of my mind, waiting for their turn. This audience was different. Some of them were more familiar than I with the passage I was reciting, and they all had the script so they could detect the smallest deviation! What would they think if I got a word wrong? Would they mind that I wasn't reading from the Bible? Would they even realize that the words I was speaking were Scripture? The weight of the risk stood on top of the difficulty of recalling memorized words and taunted me with the prospect of humiliation. However, when I should have been fearful, I was, instead, so excited for this opportunity that the fear couldn't take hold.

It went well. Not perfect, but it was a start. The recitation was well-received and smiles abounded. Honestly, though, I'm not sure that anyone was exactly sure about what had just happened.

> *Forget the former things; do not dwell on the past. See, I am doing a new thing! Now it springs up; do you not perceive it? I am making a way in the wilderness and streams in the wasteland. (Isaiah 43:18–19 NIV)*

It really was a new thing, at least it was to me. A few weeks later, Carol, Anne, and I moved from Düsseldorf, 70 km south, to Bonn, Germany, and soon started attending an international church there. We loved everything about the community and our church family. However, once again, the lay Scripture readings were less of a riveting message and more of a chance to orient oneself to the environment, to read the bulletin, and to deliver any last-minute whispered messages.

I asked if I could be one of the readers. After a few days, the response came that there was an opening in about a month. It would be the story of the feeding of the five thousand from Matthew chapter 14.

That was good news for two reasons. The first reason was that it's a great passage, and the second reason was that I would need that time to prepare. This church was bigger than the first, and I felt that the stakes were higher. At two months old, Annie stayed receptive to serving as my audience, and I repeated the words of Matthew 14 to her *ad nauseam*.

The day for the recitation came. The stage had two podiums, one on the right (as you face the stage) and one on the left. I stood behind the podium on the left and announced the passage, and then took a step to the side and began to recite the story of the feeding of the five thousand. As I did so, I noticed that there were no bulletins being read, no fidgeting, and no whispers to be heard. We were all locked in on the story. My nerves were somewhere else. I felt like a spectator to my own recitation, and I could enjoy and marvel as Jesus startled everyone, saying:

> *They do not need to go away. You give them something to eat.* (*Matthew 14:16 NIV*)

I looked directly at these wonderful people and the words from my mouth were, "*You* give them something to eat."

There were, and still are, many words that come out of my mouth, but being able to speak words so powerful and beautiful, words that cut to the core of my audience's heart and my own conscience, is something that words can't describe.

I hope that you will be in such a position and know the feeling. You will need to invest the time to memorize Scripture, to study and understand its meaning, and to place it so deeply in your heart and mind that it spills out when you exhale, and then speak it to one, or two, or a few hundred. That is when you will know the stunning clarity of the message.

The loaves and fish were distributed, and leftovers were gathered. I finished speaking, and the pastor, a beloved man who had been popular on the radio as well as from the pulpit in the United States, recognized that something special had just happened. There was a moment of quiet, and then he said, "Well, I guess we just pray and go home, because *that* was the message."

In the years that followed, after we returned to California, I would recite at our church as frequently as possible. The response was always positive. People would describe how the recitation "brought the passage to life" and inspired deeper understanding. They liked hearing the Word spoken clearly and with passion—but there was one more thing that was frequently added to the comments. It was a phrase that was something like, "*You* have a special gift. I could never do that."

I soaked up the praise and patted myself on the back until one day, when my pride had dropped its guard and I was vulnerable to thinking clearly, two thoughts came to me. The first was that, despite what people said, I *didn't* have a special gift, I just worked *really hard* to memorize these passages. And the second was that I was the excuse that allowed others to not participate in reciting. I was a hindrance to them because they could enjoy the recitation without introducing the idea that they should do it themselves. It didn't matter that I enjoyed reciting, what mattered was that I wasn't encouraging others. Over the course of the next week, the thought penetrated my thick outer crust and settled in as a decision to change course. My goal was no longer to deliver more and more recitations, my goal was to encourage and support others in having the recitation experience. That was when the recitation ministry began.

I am poorly equipped to write a book on recitation. Memorizing text is difficult for me, and the thought of standing in front of a large group of people makes my stomach queasy. In a discussion of theology, I am either unaware or uninterested. And yet, this one thing, standing in front of a group of people and speaking by heart the words of the Bible, is my joy. There are some friends in my life who are far too good for me. They're magnificent people who should not be associated with people like me. It's an honor to know them and a privilege to call them friends. Reciting Scripture is like that. I get to be associated with something so much more than who I am. It's astounding to realize, when you are reciting Scripture, that the holy God of the universe is speaking through you to the people he loves. You are standing at the interface, and the message is flowing through you. If you have a moment to dwell on a thought, dwell on that one. It won't take away the anxiousness, the sweaty palms, or the hours spent memorizing, but it will give you the perspective that what you're doing is of consequence.

MY RECITATION STORY: TIM PORTER

Tim Porter

Doing recitations is always a pleasure for me. I enjoy reciting passages from the Bible mostly because it forces me to be on a regular schedule with memorizing Scripture. I go over the same passage many hundreds of times in the days and weeks prior to the actual recitation. Sometimes, I discover something in a verse or realize its true meaning for me after *a week or so* of studying it! I feel like the Lord often reveals something to me only *after* it has rolled through my mind dozens of times. The truth is that I go through stretches where I keep up with scripture memorization and stretches where I let it drop, which are always regretful. My spiritual health is always in much better shape when I stay consistent.

The real gain for me personally is always in the study leading up to the recitation. But reciting Scripture also makes me feel like I'm contributing to the overall message being delivered by the worship team and teaching pastor, which is a good thing.

3

Recitation Discipleship

The focus of discipleship groups is to develop disciples of Christ. A recitation discipleship group is no different in that regard. If you're not familiar with discipleship groups, they are Christ-centered small teams of people committed to progressing each other on a path toward spiritual maturity. The groups are intentional in purpose, individualized in application, and involved in the church life and community.

A recitation discipleship group uses the recitation as its vehicle. Preparing for a recitation is an accelerated journey through the phases of discipleship. Whereas a typical discipleship cycle may last four-to-six months with weekly meetings, a typical recitation preparation is shorter, typically lasting one-to-two months, with three-to-five meetings.

A discipleship group will have a topic and a goal. For recitation discipleship groups, the topic is the passage to be recited, and the goal has all to do with one's progress as a disciple of Christ and making strides towards spiritual maturity. I should repeat: The goal of a recitation discipleship group is to progress participants along a path of discipleship and maturity. The goal is not the performance.

There are four stages to the recitation discipleship group, and within the stages are a varying number of meetings, depending on the complexities of the passage and the characteristics of the participants.

Stage 1—Trust Building

The recitation discipleship group consists of at least three people. If it's a solo recitation, that means bringing another person along. There is good reason for the third person.

> Though one may be overpowered, two can defend themselves. A cord of three strands is quickly broken.
>
> Ecclesiastes 4:12 NIV

Three perspectives for a Bible study, three perspectives for interpreting Scripture, three people each with unique faith walks.

We embark on the journey by getting to know about each other. Our activities include:

o   sharing our faith stories
o   setting expectations and growth goals
o   introduction to the passage

We don't dive directly into the topic, but first take time to understand each other and to define our goals and commitment for this discipleship group. Some of the most interesting information comes in this first session.

Stage 2—Learning

There's no recitation without words, and, also, no recitation without a grasp of what the words *mean*. The next stage of the discipleship begins the infusion of understanding into the passage so that, when the reciter is speaking, there will be clarity of communication.

The recitation ministry is unique in many ways, including how we go about studying the Bible. There's a clear focus in each step of the learning process that it should not only prepare us for the recitation, but it should also have a personal application. We study the passage so that we can accurately and faithfully bring it to life, as well as live it out in our own lives.

When studying for recitation, we are less interested in the influence the passage has had on the church and more interested in the moment that the words came to life. We are more interested in the original intent of the passage, the relationship of the speaker to the audience, the tone of the passage, and the circumstances or events that necessitated the words to be written.

As with other Bible studies, we want to apply the lessons that we glean into our lives, and then invest those lessons in others.

While remembering that these are sweeping generalizations, a comparison of a recitation Bible study with a traditional Bible study is shown below.

Traditional Bible Study	Recitation Bible Study
Understand how to apply the passage moving forward	Understand what *prompted* the passage to be printed in the first place
Explore the range of possible meanings of a passage	Decide on the *one* tone and texture of the passage that will be recited
Define the syntax of the words of the passage	Define how the words of the passage will be voiced
Identifying word etymology to understand connections to other passages	Identifying word prompts and cues that will trigger recall

A recitation Bible study analyzes the passage through four perspectives—participants, tone, words, and anchors.

A. Participants

1. Who was the writer's audience and how are they similar and different to your audience?
2. Who is the speaker and how is he or she similar and different from you?
3. What was the relationship of the author to the audience and how is that similar and different to the relationship of you to your audience?

B. Tone

Tone is the overarching feel of a passage. Was it an angry criticism, a joyful praise, a disciplined teaching? Was it the tone of a father to a child, a teacher to a student, a philosopher, or a worshipper? We pursue two questions in discussing tone.

1. What is the attitude of the message?
2. Which words are key to conveying the tone?

C. Word Selection

The particular word choice depends on the version of the Bible that you have selected, but behind the word is the meaning it's meant to convey. Words can be pejorative or delightful. The same word may have multiple meanings, and the choice between two words that have the same meaning bends the tone of the passage and affects the message.

When we look at word selection, we look not only for the

qualities of the words, but, for a recitation, we also have some very practical considerations.

1. Which words are difficult to pronounce?
2. Which words do you need to clearly define?
3. Which words are similar to each other?
   o Similar words can cause confusion. Pick them out and work on creating distinctions.

D. Anchors (safe-haven verses)

Safe havens are the verses within your passage in which you have supreme confidence. When you reach a safe haven, you're in a place of confidence. Safe havens also serve as reference points that locate you within the passage. From the safe haven, you know which portions are already past and which are still to come. These verses will serve as your anchors, not only in your initial memorization, but also during the recitation itself. Take time to know these verses inside and out, so that when you land on them, you'll find refuge. For more information about safe-haven verses, see chapter 6.

Stage 3—Synthesis

At the synthesis stage, the pieces come together, and the text begins to become the message. There's now meaning to the passage and a sense of the tone and rhythm. It's time for you to begin to apply the passage, both to the onstage delivery of your recitation as well as to the incorporation of the lessons gleaned from the passage into your life.

During onstage rehearsals, you'll start to feel comfortable onstage. It should also be a time for you to incorporate stage movements (blocking) that coordinate with the meaning of the passage. When done correctly, stage motions will also provide you with physical cues for aiding your memory recall.

Putting the words into action onstage is a great analogy to putting the words into action in one's life. What have you learned from the passage that can make an immediate impact in how you handle your daily challenges?

The synthesis stage ends with the delivery of your recitation.

Stage 4–Discipling Others

One of the commitments when being led to recite should include a goal to subsequently lead someone else through the process.

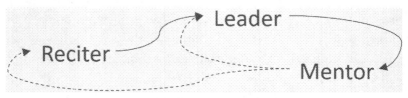

Progression from Reciter to Mentor

How soon you'll be ready to take that next step in leading a reciter depends on your personal progress and maturity. It may take just one round of preparing to recite, and then delivering a recitation, to also prepare you to subsequently lead someone else through the preparation process. However, a successful recitation is not the key indicator. The most important indicator is your heart and whether you have a desire to help someone else through the process.

While not everyone will be immediately ready to lead others through the process of preparing to recite, the expectation of embarking on a recitation discipleship group is one of continual growth. The shape of that growth will depend on your walk with the Lord. Your next step in growth may be a different type of recitation—for example, if you recited a Psalm, maybe next time recite a teaching from one of the epistles, or an historical account—or it may be a different type of discipleship group. Your growth as a disciple of Christ is the goal.

Reciting, and leading others to recite, makes us stronger in the Word and in the depth of our relationships. In the discipleship model, growth will always extend out to nourish others in the body of Christ.

> So Christ himself gave the apostles, the prophets, the evangelists, the pastors and teachers, to equip his people for works of service, so that the body of Christ may be built up until we all reach unity in the faith and in the knowledge of the Son of God and mature, attaining to the whole measure of the fullness of Christ.
>
> Ephesians 4:11–13 NIV

Prayerfully consider to whom you would extend an invitation. Who could you invest time in to help them disciple through recitation? We all benefit from the recitation experience. It's one means of nourishing the body of Christ and making one another more alive for service in God's Kingdom.

4

Guiding Principles for Reciters

And I will take the blind by a way of which they
had no knowledge, guiding them by roads strange
to them: I will make the dark places light before
them, and the rough places level.

Isaiah 42:16 BBE

The Basic Principles of Reciting

It may, indeed, feel to someone who has never recited like a road
"strange to them." You may feel a bit, or maybe a lot, outside of
your comfort zone. That's a common feeling. In reciting, the playing
field is perfectly level, the same whether you're a child or a CEO.
You may think it is *unfairly* level, but it's a fact that your social
status or bank account will gain you no advantage when it comes
to reciting. Perhaps the most daunting thing about standing in
front of hundreds of people and reciting is the feeling that you're
not in control. There are many factors at work. The room may be
hot or cold. The people may be few or many, focused or distracted,
content or crying, squirmy or still, well-behaved or mischievous—
and that's just the adults. And then there is that imperfect recall
device positioned behind our eyes that's just waiting to be distracted

by a flash of light or a pop of sound, a stray thought, or a squeaky shoe. Throw in the sound of your amplified voice, and the unusual perspective of having so many faces looking at you, and it's no wonder that you would feel some anxiety at the prospect of reciting.

There are four principles that have naturally evolved to support the process of recitation. Each has its foundation in one goal—keeping you, the reciter, in charge.

1—You Choose the Version

If you're going to spend weeks memorizing a sizable passage, including devoting free time to the task, exploring the structure and definitions, and endlessly repeating the passage, then it makes sense that you, the reciter, get to choose the Bible version to which you will be devoting so much intellectual capital.

There's such a range of choices. Many choose NIV or ESV. Some of our reciters use the KJV exclusively and can speak it so clearly and fluidly that it doesn't feel like you're in the fifteenth century. However unusual the sentence structure may be compared to modern language, there are some passages that just sound so beautiful in that old-fashioned language that I wouldn't want to hear it any other way.

Your choice of version may be based on personal significance. Perhaps a passage was read at your baptism in a particular version or is traditionally read in a certain version by your family. You may also consider who your audience will be. Will you be reciting to children or adults? To a primarily un-churched group, or to faithful believers?

Choose the version that you love and feel will best communicate the message from you. You'll be spending quite a bit of time with the passage, so you should adore it.

2—You Get Time to Prepare

There are no "rush job" recitations. It's not about the performance. If you're unclear about that, you should reread the first part of chapter 2. The goal of a recitation discipleship group is to progress disciples along their faith path. Most of the good that is done is accomplished in the preparation leading up to the day of recitation. There's far more to the recitation than memorizing words, and you need time to prepare. You must be thinking months in advance to plan your preparation time, taking into account holidays, vacation plans, special events, and business schedules, not only planning the day of the recitation, but also the rehearsals leading up to the day.

Whether it's your first recitation or your fiftieth, it takes time. As a guideline, it takes at least a month to prepare to recite. You should add to that time for any extenuating circumstances that would delay the process. Be forewarned, applying the college-student technique of cramming for an exam should not be used for a recitation. It doesn't work. It leaves you vulnerable onstage and actually defeats the purpose of doing the recitation in the first place. It's better to delay the recitation date than to make this marvelous journey into a burdensome task.

3—You Decide on When

There will be a target date for the recitation. The date keeps you focused and motivated. Often, it's meant to coincide with a specific teaching, a scheduled worship song, or a service theme. However, in the end, it's you, the reciter, who will decide if it's the right time. If the date comes and you're not ready, then don't recite. If the date comes and you are ill or have experienced a trauma or there is anything that would steal your joy in reciting, then don't do it. It's the preparation, the hours spent practicing and refining your recitation, that are the gold. During that time, you will have been an example to your family and friends of how important the Word is to you. Not only to others—it also bears witness to you, revealing your heart to yourself. A reciter should always have the final say.

> "At any time, right up to the day of the planned recitation, if you feel it will do you more harm than good to recite, then don't. By that time, 95 percent of the good has already been done."

The purpose to this third principle is to take some pressure off you. No announcements about the recitation coming in the next weeks, no line of people telling you how they're looking forward to hearing your recitation, and not even a mention in the bulletin on the day of the recitation. You can decide who should know in advance. You should always feel that you're in charge, and that the recitation comes from a sense of eager anticipation and not dreaded duty. The motivation for this guideline is that you will be feeling enough pressure as it is, and a throng of well-wishers will just add to the pressure.

4—You Will Be Supported

My father-in-law would frequently share some good West Virginian wisdom based on an old proverb, "There's many a slip 'twixt the cup and the lip."

The meaning is that even when you have a sure thing in your hand, a cup of some beverage right in front of you, and you just need to raise it to your lips and drink, things can still go wrong. Your elbow may be jostled, your fingers slide on the handle, or you just miss your mouth. Some of that beverage is now dampening your shirt or pants and dripping to the floor. What seemed to have been a sure thing is now a mess.

This was my reality on one summer Sunday while reciting Isaiah 53.

For our transgressions, he was crushed for our iniquities; the punishment that brought us peace was on him, and by his wounds we are healed. We all, like sheep, have gone astray, each of us has turned to our own way. (Isaiah 53:5–6 NIV)

It happened between verses 5 and 6, when there's a shift in the focus of the passage from Jesus to us, from "by his wounds we are healed" to "we all, like sheep." After the word *healed*, I paused. Then, I heard the air conditioner click on.

Now, the air conditioner had been part of the building remodel when this former Volkswagen technical center had become our church home. We had been meeting in schools, and after years of setting up and taking down the church every Sunday, we finally had a solid home. The air conditioner was a heavy unit that rested on the roof. In addition, the lights and speakers were intended to hang from the ceiling, so it had been necessary to add reinforcement to the roof in order to bear the load.

The air conditioner's *click* triggered all these memories about how far we had come since the church had been planted almost eight years before. The memory that it did *not* trigger was what comes after "by his wounds we are healed."

I was at a loss. The bridge was washed out. The spare tire was flat. The emergency chute hadn't been packed. I had absolutely no idea what the next words were, even though I'd repeatedly rehearsed this passage perfectly. The silence was pervasive.

And then a voice from the back right side of the audience said, "We all, like sheep," and I continued with "have gone astray." It was all I needed. I had been rescued from the abyss. Ken Bailey had been following along in his Bible and had realized that I needed a prompt. I am ever grateful to Ken for giving me those four words. And the irony of going off-track just before the words "we all, like sheep, have gone astray" was not lost on me. It was an invaluable lesson.

That's why there's always someone "on book" during a recitation.

Always. Even the most amazing reciter, someone with an eidetic memory, theological training, and years of experience, can get "vapor lock," struggling onstage to find the words that have come so easily dozens of times before. The person "on book" is a lifeline. It only takes a couple of words to get a reciter back in the groove.

The person "on book" will sit in the front row and do nothing but watch the words of the text. When you're reciting and there's a pause, then the on-book person will look up. If you're looking elsewhere, then it's just a dramatic pause. If you're looking at the on-book person, then you will be prompted with the next few words, spoken loudly. The words of the prompt are projected forward, toward the reciter at the front, so the rest of the audience rarely even knows what has just happened.

It's good to "practice making a mistake" with your on-book person, just so that you and the prompter are in tune with one another if a slip-up happens. Don't leave this to chance. During rehearsals, pretend to need a prompt, and then the on-book person should practice providing the prompt. Make sure that you are in sync on this so that you're ready in case it happens. In early-stage rehearsals, the prompts may not need to be pretend, as you are still getting familiar with the passage and you'll need some prompting. This is also a good example of why rehearsing early in the preparation process is a benefit.

Still, it's best to practice and practice. Don't just practice until you get it right, practice until you can't get it wrong.

MY RECITATION STORY: CONNIE JOHNSON

Connie Johnson

I've never enjoyed getting up in front of an audience. Ironically, when I was young, I recall doing Bible memory verses in front of my church, but as I grew older, I was less and less inclined to do it. So when I was asked to participate in a Scripture recitation, I wasn't willing. Though I memorize Scripture regularly and strongly believe in the importance of memorizing passages, I wanted to leave the recitations to others.

However, after numerous invitations, I eventually felt that I could no longer avoid the inevitable. I knew that for me to refuse again and again to get up in front of the church to recite Scriptures—due to my own vanity and nervousness—was disobedience. I wanted to obey God even if it was uncomfortable. So I agreed to recite on the condition that I could do it with a friend. Just having another person beside you on stage is comforting. The other confidence booster for me was "overmemorizing" the passage. Being very prepared takes a lot of the nervousness out of public speaking. It also helped that I had a very kind, patient, and encouraging director.

5

Choosing a Passage to Recite

There are four steps in the process for a reciter, and it begins when you select a passage to recite.

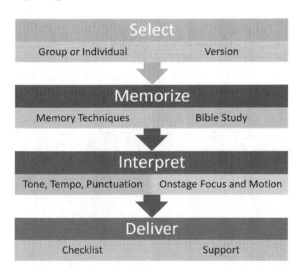

Find a passage that conveys one idea. For some passages, that means one or two verses. For other passages, it may be an entire chapter or more. It doesn't need to be a huge passage. Some recitations are short, clear, and powerful.

You may have seen or heard about performances of an entire book of the Bible, and that's a marvelous feat that can be inspiring.

However, the recitations that we're describing in this book are not meant to be impressive or marvelous. They're meant to be clear messages. Consequently, there's a limit to how large a recited passage should be. There are two dangers to crossing the size boundary. The first danger is that the response to it may be more about how impressive the feat was, rather than how beautiful or meaningful the passage was. The second danger is that it may be too much for the audience to absorb in one sitting, so they start to tune out from the recitation. If you're considering memorizing an entire book, that's great, please do so—but when it comes to reciting, do so in comprehensible portions.

The passage that you choose to recite can be based on who you naturally are. Your nature may be that you like to tell stories, or you may like to teach or to sing praises to God. Your preference may change from one time to the next. If you know that you would like to recite, but don't have a specific passage in mind, then it's easiest to start the process by selecting from three broad groups—stories, teachings, or praise. The examples shown below are arranged in these groups and further broken into sub-groups. One example is shown for each subgroup. The groups are meant to facilitate consideration and are not meant as an exhaustive categorization scheme.

Stories

- Acts of Faith—1 Kings 18:22–40 NIV: "Choose one of the bulls and prepare it first, since there are so many of you. Call on the name of your god, but do not light the fire."
- Prophecy—Isaiah 53:1–12 NIV: "He took up our pain and bore our suffering, yet we considered him punished by God, stricken by him, and afflicted. But he was pierced for our transgressions."

Teaching

- Admonishment and Worldly Influence—James 2:14–26 ESV: "And one of you says to them, 'Go in peace, be warmed and filled,' without giving them the things needed for the body, what good is that?"
- Christian Walk—1Peter 3:15–16 NIV: "Be prepared to give an answer to everyone who asks you to give the reason for the hope that you have."

Praise

- God's Love for Us—Isaiah 43:1–7 NIV: "When you pass through the waters, I will be with you; and when you pass through the rivers."
- Person and Deity of Christ—Colossians 1:13–20 NIV: "The Son is the image of the invisible God, the firstborn over all creation. For in him all things were created: things in heaven and on earth, visible and invisible."
- Praise—Psalm 27:4–5 NIV: "One thing I ask from the Lord, this only do I seek: that I may dwell in the house of the Lord all the days of my life."

Further examples are provided in the appendix of this book.

Group Recitations

Most commonly, a recitation is a solo event, meaning one person reciting one passage. If there was nothing else, that would be more than enough. However, there are additional ways of presenting Scripture that includes multiple passages or groups of people.

You may decide that you would like to join a group recitation. These take on many forms that highlight the depth, diversity, consistency, and beauty of the Word. They are also a wonderful chance to get to extend your circle of friends in fellowship as you work together preparing to recite. A unique and lasting camaraderie develops, as you depend on each other in a stressful situation.

An example of a group recitation is Daniel 3:1–18 in which Daniel's friends are threatened with being thrown into the fiery furnace. In short, they refuse. Recited by three siblings, the passage matched their natural chemistry. Another example is Psalm 51:1–12, the psalm of confession and mercy, recited by nine people in nine different languages. This pairing did well in reflecting the universal need for confession and forgiveness.

Please refer to the additional examples of group recitations that are provided in the sister book to this, *The Art of Leading Scripture Reciters.*

6

Memorization Techniques

Do you have the ability to easily memorize large blocks of text? Some people do—but the rest of us need to invest a lot of work, and we can use some assistance! If you're like me, you may like some help in succeeding at this first step in preparing to recite. Following are some techniques specifically aimed at reciters.

Practice Out Loud

This technique is for all forms of recitation, whether they are long or short, individual or group. It's always effective and necessary when it comes to memorizing for a recitation. Practice *out loud*. Practice at full volume if you can, but even if it's whispered while the rest of your household is asleep, it makes a difference to hear the words and start to grapple with how they should be voiced. The sooner you get to the point of hearing the expression, the sooner you'll be able to identify the parts that you don't understand. Those parts should be the target of your research and prayers.

Practice out loud because some words are difficult to pronounce. Get ahead of this one. It will take time to naturally pronounce unfamiliar words correctly. It's distracting to the message if you say words incorrectly. For words that are unfamiliar, seek help in the correct pronunciation, especially names that were from a different time. Here are some difficult-to-pronounce words from the Bible.

- propitiation
- Baal (looks easy, but frequently mispronounced)
- Beelzebul or Beelzebub
- Mephibosheth
- Eluid
- Gamaliel
- Thessalonians

There's a website that helps with pronouncing Biblical words: https://www.biblespeech.com/.

Practice out loud because it's different than practicing in your head, and you're training to recite out loud. It wouldn't be a recitation if it were just in your head.

Focus Progression

Where you look when you are reciting can act as a memory prompt. Your eye progression can remind you of where you are in the passage. Something like, "When I look to the left side, I'm reciting *ABC*, and when I shift to the right side, I'm reciting *XYZ*."

Divide the audience into sections and decide where you will look when reciting.

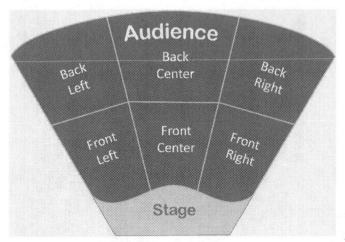

Creating reference sections in the audience for use as memory cues

For example, the story of the birth of Christ in Luke 2:1–7 NIV can be divided into four sections. The numbers, below, indicate section divisions, and do not correspond to verse numbers.

1. In those days, Caesar Augustus issued a decree that a census should be taken of the entire Roman world.
2. And everyone went to their own town to register. So Joseph also went up from the town of Nazareth in Galilee to Judea, to Bethlehem the town of David, because he belonged to the house and line of David.
3. He went there to register with Mary, who was pledged to be married to him and was expecting a child. While they were there, the time came for the baby to be born, and she gave birth to her firstborn, a son.
4. She wrapped him in cloths and placed him in a manger, because there was no guest room available for them.

If we lay this passage over the audience sections, then it might look like this.

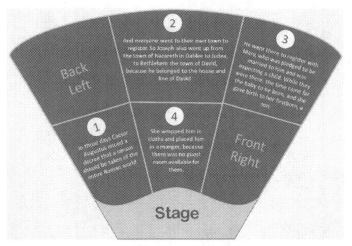

Overlay of the passage on the audience sections

The reciter then associates certain areas of the audience with specific sections of the passage. The back right is when Joseph and Mary are registering, and then the child is born. The back middle came before that, and it was the part with "everyone" (because the back middle is the largest portion of the audience, in this case) going to register.

Anchor (Safe-Haven) Verses

This technique is used when memorizing medium-to-long passages. The goal is to solidify a few "safe havens" within the passage so that, when you reach the safe haven, you'll be in a place of confidence. These verses also serve as reference points for what is already past, and what is still to come.

To do this, find one or two verses partway through the passage and take some extra time to memorize those. It could be one verse halfway through, or one verse a third of the way and a second verse two-thirds of the way. These verses will serve as your anchors, not only in your initial memorization, but also during the recitation itself. Take time to know these verses inside and out, so that when you land on them, you will find refuge. You know what has come before and what will follow, and, in the moment, you will have clarity and comfort.

Walking around the Lake

This technique involves an association between a geographical location and a section of your passage. It was described to me by a man who had memorized Psalm 139 as he'd walked around a lake near his home. Each portion was related to a feature of the lake environment. Verses 1–3 were in a sunny spot, verses 4–6 were across from a young tree located on an island in the lake, verses 7 12 near a cave, and so on. This could be an effective tool for your kit of techniques.

Patterns

Patterns fall into the category of memory aids (mnemonics).

- Create acrostics with the words of the passage. For example, the **town of N**azareth in **G**alilee - T, O, N, G is "tong," like how you "ting a tong." Memory triggers don't need to make sense, they just need to be memorable.
- Find overarching patterns in the passage. For example, the fruits of the spirit (Galatians 5:22–23 ESV) are love, joy, peace, patience, kindness, goodness, faithfulness, gentleness, self-control. There are nine. The first three are one-syllable, the second three are two-syllable, and the third three are three-syllable (1–2–3).
- Find alliteration patterns (even if they are contrived). I kept Nehemiah 6:5 NIV straight by remembering the *s* sounds throughout it. "Then, the fifth time, **S**anballat **s**ent his aide

to me with the same message, and in his hand was an unsealed letter." I'm usually terrible at remembering the address, but I knew that this was verse 5 because it was leading up to Nehemiah 6, six. Yes, I know that sounds dopey, but it works.

Bible Memory Apps

There are several apps on the market that you can use on a computer, tablet, or smartphone to help you memorize Scripture. Listed below are several popular web applications for Bible memory.

- The Bible Memory App
- Fighter Verses
- Remember Me
- Scripture Memory Fellowship (SMF)
- Verses
- The Verses Project (website)

Everyone will have their favorite memorization techniques and preferred apps. For me, the use of the Verses Bible memory app significantly reduces the amount of time it takes me to memorize a passage.

In the Verses app, you select a passage and add it to a collection. Multiple passages can be added to each collection. For longer passages, you can create subsets of the passage. For example, learning Deuteronomy 30:1–20 NIV, I added the subsets shown in the diagram to help me with transitions. Not only subsets, but also bridges or transition passages. Don't underestimate the importance of the transition verses because it's at the interface between two different thoughts, or different sentence structures, or different topics, that we usually have problems.

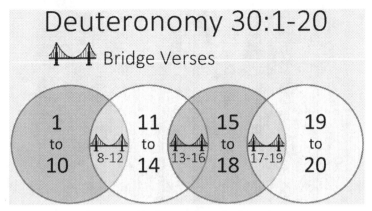

Focus on Bridge verses to link sections

For each passage, you select activities that will help you to memorize. Most apps will have some combination of activities that help you to focus and keep your attention. I like the variety of activities in the Verses app, so I'll use the Verses terminology:

Tap to Reveal–Starting with a blank screen, try to recall the first phrase (usually it's up to the first comma or period), and then tap the screen and the phrase will display. Repeat for the next phrase.

Tap to Reveal is the lowest level of interaction and contributes to the outer ring of your progress ring. It increments the outer progress ring by 10 percent, up to four times, and it does not increment the inner health ring.

Word Bank, Type Out, and Reorder views of the Verses app

Word Bank–The passage is presented on screen with some fill-in-the-blanks. At the bottom of the screen are eight candidate words. You tap the word that fills the blank. When your selection is correct, you move to the next blank. There are three levels to this activity, with progressively more blanks. In the third level, there are only blanks–but remember, you will have words from which you can choose.

Reorder–The phrases of the passage are jumbled. Drag the phrase into its correct relationship with another phrase. Continue until you have brought all of the phrases of the passage into order.

Type Out–The pinnacle. You have a blank screen, and then tap the first letter of the next word. If you are correct, the word displays, and you can move to the next word. If you're incorrect three times for any one word, then the App will display the word in red and move on.

Your progress is tracked. Every time you complete a task, a little part of your "circle" will show up. The longer you use the app and successfully memorize verses, the more complete the rings on your circle will appear. This app has a lot of variety, however, the only free version you can memorize from is the King James Version. Other versions require purchase, but it's much less expensive than a paper

Bible and far more efficient in helping you to memorize. This is a good investment.

The "Start Anywhere" Exercise

The "start anywhere" exercise is the pinnacle for a reciter because once you can do this, you're ready. I remember as Jeff was rehearsing his recitation of James 4:7–12 NIV. He was doing so well as he confidently voiced,

> Submit yourselves, then, to God. Resist the devil,
> and he will flee from you. Come near to God and
> he will come near to you. (James 4:7–8 NIV)

And then he stopped. He hesitated a moment, and then said, "Let me start over." My response startled even me. "No, you never get to do that." I prompted him with the next few words, and he continued.

When there's a hiccup in a recitation, you don't get to go back and start over. You must be able to recognize phrases and be able to pick up in the middle. "Start anywhere" prepares you for this.

You'll need an assistant. It could be anyone, from your discipleship group leader, to your child, to the person standing in line with you at the coffee shop. The assistant reads a short phrase from the passage, and the reciter then continues from that point for a short time. Then the assistant finds another point in the passage and reads a short phrase with the reciter then continuing from that point. The selections should be randomly selected. The only thing to watch for is if a phrase occurs exactly the same in more than one place in the passage. The reciter must be given enough information to distinguish which part of the passage is the source of their prompt.

Mastering the "start anywhere" is a huge confidence builder and an indicator of preparedness.

MY RECITATION STORY: JEFF NORTON

Jeff Norton

My first recitation was Acts 20:28–32 NIV ("Be on your guard"). Reciting really made the passage come alive for me, as I had to put myself in Paul's shoes and speak to his people as him! Memorizing scriptures before that really didn't motivate me much. There were some that I had memorized because they were important, oft read, or just easy–but not as a consistent discipline. But that really changed when I recited. It was like God's hand was on me. It wasn't onerous or difficult. It was exciting. I was the narrator. I was Paul. I was John. Whoever was speaking, it was like I was them in the moment, speaking to their audience. It wasn't really reciting so much as it was me talking to them as I imagined Paul or John would have. It was reciting in the sense that it was word-for-word, but the more I got to know it, the more I became the person speaking as he would ordinarily speak, no longer repeating words from rote memorization.

The other thing that impressed me and that I try to pass on to reciters and potential reciters is that there are levels of knowing. At the first level, you can recite the passage for yourself. You get to the point where you don't stumble or search for the next word, you know it cold and can confidently recite the whole passage.

Then, you do it for someone else. Suddenly, everything is shaky again, and you realize you don't really know it to the level you need. So you keep working on it until you can confidently recite and engage with your audience. Reciting for others takes another step all by itself but engaging with the audience in particular brings it to a whole new level. Aha! Now you think you really have it.

Then, you practice it up front in the sanctuary. Suddenly, everything is shaky again, and you realize you don't really know it to the level you need. So you keep working on it until you can do that. Now, you're at what I call level three. There's still another level to come, doing it live up there in front of the whole congregation. You don't get any practices on this one, so you must rely on your preparation. If you've prepared well through the first three levels, you can usually make it to this fourth level. At the least, you should be able to recite confidently while keeping the congregation out of your mind. If you achieved mastery, you can actually engage with the congregation as you recite. This is more difficult, as you have to focus on them and be confident the words will come rather than focusing on the words. It has to pour forth from within you. But when you can do it, it's like God is pouring his words into their hearts, and you get to be the conduit!

7

Biblical Interpretation

Once the text is memorized, then the real work begins to reveal the message. Your goal is to make the moment when this passage took its first breath come to life. To do so, you must understand what the author's intent was in putting pen to paper. In this chapter, we'll discuss Biblical interpretation, or *hermeneutics*. When interpreting Scripture, you need to understand the author's intention and not apply your own bias. The interpretation must make sense in the context of the passages surrounding it and in relation to the audience for whom it was intended. Before you can recite the passage, you must understand the interpretation. Only then will you be able to animate the passage.

Although it may sound beatnik to say, it's true that the most important aspect for an effective recitation is the tone and tempo of the message. How you express the message is as important as the words themselves. Tone and tempo, however, must have their foundations in an accurate understanding of the passage with its intended meaning. This chapter is an example of the inductive Bible study method—as it applies to preparing for a recitation. Although the focus in this book is about expressing the message, and there are additional time-consuming activities that must be accomplished in preparation for a recitation, you cannot neglect the centrality of a thoughtful and focused academic Bible study in order to arrive at some specific answers about how you will express the message.

First observe, and then interpret. Answering the following six questions will culminate in an accurate observation and provide for a firm foundation to interpret the message that you will be delivering. We divide the six observation questions into two sections; first, we answer the observation questions, and then we address the final two observation questions, which bridge the gap between observation and interpretation.

Observation

Who?

People are at the core of our relationships. To understand the people involved on all sides of the equation is critical to understanding the passage. Are they believers? Young or old? Sick or well? Persecuted or free? Homogenous or disparate? The "who" questions boil down to:

- Who is speaking?
- Who is the recipient of the letter?
- Who is being spoken about?

The people within the passage have a relationship of some sort. How close is the writer connected to the audience? Friends, acquaintances, previously unknown to one another? Is it an authoritative relationship or chummy? Do they have a history together? Define their identity. Is it a national identity, a cultural identity, a familial identity?

Explore the characteristics of these people because how you speak to them depends on who they are—their heritage as well as their current standing.

What?

The *what* gets us to the core of the action. Find the verbs, and they will make you see the connection between intention and result. Refrain from drawing conclusions yet. This stage is all about seeing clearly, eyes wide open. Search for answers to the "what" questions:

- What is (are) the subject(s)?
- What is (are) the object(s)?
- What is being said about them?

When?

Look for any time clues in the passage. These may be references that sequence the events described in the passage or references to historical events such as in Isaiah 6:1 ("In the year that King Uzziah died"). When you can define the time period of events in the passage, then you will have more ammunition for an accurate interpretation because each time period has its own characteristics.

- Is there any clear sense of past, present, and/or future?
- When did (will) the event(s) take place?
- Are temporal (time) aspects found in the text?

Where?

The characteristics of a time period are brought into focus as you understand the location. The cultural characteristics of a location are contained within a time/place box. When you can visualize the location involved in the passage then you will find new meaning in the words and the message.

- Do specific locations appear in the text (Jerusalem, Antioch, Babylon)?
- Do general locations appear (mountains, sky, city)?

Connect Observation to Interpretation

The last two questions connect us to the interpretation, acting as a bridge between observations and interpretation

How?

This speaks to the issue of the means by which something is accomplished. It assumes that an action happened and that the author chose to tell us about how it took place.

Why?

Find the motivating factors for the actions expressed in the passage. Knowing the people, location, and time period will help you to understand the reasons involved.

- Is a reason given for a specific act?
- Does an action have a specific intended purpose?

Interpretation

Once you have made your observations, then you will move on to interpretation, which seeks to answer the broad question, "What does the author mean by what he says?" Assuming that we deal with a single paragraph (in the epistles) or section (in the narrative writings), the interpretation process begins with two broad issues. We arrive at our interpretation by developing a subject and complement for our text.

Subject

First, identify the primary idea the author addresses. How would one state the key thought of the paragraph? Some call this the *subject* of the paragraph, and it answers the question, "What is the author writing about?"

Complement

Second, having identified what the author writes about, now one looks to answer the question, "What does the author say about what he is writing about?" This is often called the *complement* to the subject.

Taken together, the subject and complement form the main idea that summarizes what the passage says and means. At this point you have achieved the most fundamental step in interpretation!

Mechanisms

Use the following four mechanisms to refine and test the validity of your interpretation.

1. Distinguish the primary and significant truths from subordinate truths.
2. Determine a title that summarizes the text's most important concept.
3. Outline the text based on the subject and complement.
4. Paraphrase the entire text (i.e., put it into your own words).

A Worked Example using Psalm 1:1–6 ESV

The best way to show this method is to work out an example. This example will examine Psalm 1:1–6 ESV, first defining the observations, and then drawing the interpretation.

> *Psalm 1:1*: *"Blessed is the man who walks not in the counsel of the wicked, nor stands in the way of sinners, nor sits in the seat of scoffers."*

> *Psalm 1:2*: *"But his delight is in the law of the* Lord, *and on his law he meditates day and night."*

> *Psalm 1:3*: *"He is like a tree planted by streams of water that yields its fruit in its season, and its leaf does not wither. In all that he does, he prospers."*

> *Psalm 1:4*: *"The wicked are not so, but are like chaff that the wind drives away."*

> *Psalm 1:5*: *"Therefore the wicked will not stand in the judgment, nor sinners in the congregation of the righteous."*

> *Psalm 1:6*: *"For the* Lord *knows the way of the righteous, but the way of the wicked will perish."*

Observation Worksheet: A Worked Example using Psalm 1:1–6 ESV

Who?

- Who is writing? David
- Who is speaking? David

- Who is the recipient of the letter? All people
- Who is being spoken about? The blessed man (vv. 1–3, 6); the wicked man (vv. 4–5, 6); the Lord (vv. 2, 6)

What?

What is (are) the subject(s)? The blessed man is described in three ways (all in the negative) in verse 1. He is described as one who delights in the Lord's law and who meditates on it (v. 2). This blessed man is likened to a tree that is nourished by water, produces fruit at the right time, and whose leaf does not wither; a life of prosperity (v. 3). The wicked are contrasted with the blessed (v. 4), especially in regard to prosperity! The wicked are like chaff driven and dispersed by the wind (v. 4).

When?

- Is there any clear sense of past, present, and/or future? The majority of statements describe present realities in the form of characteristic behavior or state of being for both the blessed (vv. 1–3) and the wicked (v. 4). The author refers to the future final judgment of the wicked (vv. 5–6).
- When did (will) the event(s) take place? No specific time.
- Are temporal (time) aspects found in the text? The time begins in the relative past ("a tree planted") and ends in the future ("will not stand"). There is relative time ("in its season") and continuous ("day and night") (v. 2).

Where?

- Do specific locations appear in the text (Jerusalem, Antioch, Babylon)? No.

- Do general locations appear (mountains, sky, city)? Streams of water (v. 3).

Connect Observation to Interpretation: Worked Example using Psalm 1:1–6 ESV

How?

- This speaks to the issue of the means by which something is accomplished. It assumes that an action happened and that the author chose to tell us how it took place.
  The author gives three negative statements of how the blessed man does *not* live (v. 1) in contrast to his involvement with the Law of God (v. 2).

Why?

- Is a reason given for a specific act?
  Planting a tree is done for a purpose; to enjoy its fruit, or its shade, or its beauty. There is an act of judgment.
- Does an action have a specific intended purpose?
  o yield fruit (v. 3)
  o judgment to remove the wicked (vv. 4, 6)

Interpretation: Worked Example using Psalm 1:1–6 ESV

Subject

The contrast between the blessed person and the wicked person.

Complement

The blessed one takes his direction in life from God's law, not from the wicked (vv. 1–2); and he anticipates the benefits of such a life, not pending judgment (vv. 3–6).

Mechanisms

- Distinguish the primary and significant truths from subordinate truths.
  With the brevity of Psalm 1, few subordinate truths exist.
- Determine a title that summarizes the text's most important concept.
  Two Lives Contrasted: the Blessed Versus the Wicked
- Outline the text based on the subject and complement.
  o The blessed and the wicked look to different sources for direction in life (vv. 1–2).
  o The blessed and the wicked anticipate vastly different outcomes (vv. 3–6).

- Paraphrase the entire text (i.e., put it into your own words). Great benefit comes to the person who does not pursue "wisdom" from those who do not follow God (1); on the contrary, this one is thrilled with and devotes himself to the pursuit of God's law (2). This blessed person receives nourishment from such a lifestyle, and thereby grows and produces fruit in consequence of his living (3).
  The opposite, the wicked, produce a life of instability and "throwaways," while facing the certainty of a bad day of judgment before God (4–5, 6). Because God knows the blessed to be different, their prospects of judgment produce confidence (6).

8

Animating a Passage

A common misperception is that a reciter is like a show business actor. This couldn't be further from the truth.

If you've ever tuned a guitar or have seen a piano tuner, then you're familiar with comparing to a reference and adjusting until the dissonance disappears. The string tension is adjusted until its vibration matches the reference tone, and when it matches, the sound intensifies and purifies. It is "in tune." Tuning a stringed instrument isn't about extremes. You don't make the string as tight as possible or as loose as possible; you adjust its tension until it's at its harmonious "somewhere in the middle."

We have the same tuning in our lives. We find the balance point between hoarding all worldly goods and giving them all away; the balance between work and play, between huddling with friends and reaching out to strangers. Our lives are filled with these dynamic tensions for which there just isn't an extreme answer. We are meant to walk the straight path, which is a balance. Every day, we must find the balance point.

And so it is with a recitation. It's a balance. Monotone or quavering? Dressed in drab gray or sophisticated costume? Surrounded by sterile walls or elaborate props? Stock still or dramatic?

The answer will depend on your recitation, but generally, it's somewhere in the middle—a sincere voice using gestures that we use every day by which we communicate. The balance point is where the message that you're delivering matches who you are. Acting is about being somebody other than yourself. Recitation is about being completely you. When every part of you—your voice, your motions, and your emotions match the message, then you are "in tune." That is *not* an act!

If you understand the author's intent, then you'll translate that into how you will convey that same message, being true to the original intent.

In our section on interpretation (chapter 7), we started with understanding who the audience was and what the author's relationship was to the audience. They lived in unique circumstances within a defined society. When you can connect the text with the people, relationships, circumstances, and society, you'll begin to understand the message. When you understand the message, then the appropriate tone, tempo, and punctuation will rise to the surface. The message will be conveyed in a manner that matches both the reciter and the intent of the passage.

Tone, tempo, and inflection can bend a passage in a certain direction. Was the speaker teaching? Encouraging? Counseling? Read the following:

> Behold, I stand at the door and knock; if anyone
> hears My voice and opens the door, I will come in
> to him and will dine with him, and he with Me.
>
> Revelation 3:20 NASB

Is the intent to extend an invitation to an outsider, or is it demanding discipline from a group of believers?

Your answer will determine how you recite this passage. You may recite it as a sweet invitation to dine with the king, or you may recite it as a stern rebuke to a church that has left him out on the street.

Discuss the possible interpretations in your discipleship group but understand that you must eventually decide on one and only one interpretation. There's only one answer for the reciter, and it can take months of living with the passage and researching before it's clear. This is another reason that we allow a long time for preparation. The work isn't just in knowing the words; it's knowing how to say them.

The interpretation of a passage is a good time to involve your pastor in the discussion either to help you understand how to interpret the passage or to validate your proposed interpretation.

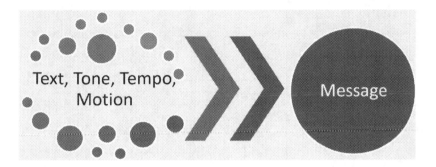

Accurate delivery of the message will depend on how well you understand it, and to do this, you'll need to "get inside" the message. A Bible study is a good starting point.

We have already discussed the recitation Bible study designed to accompany recitations (chapter 3). The purpose of the Bible study is to analyze the passage through four perspectives (participants, tone, words, and anchors) and seeks to answer the questions: "What was in the heart of the author?" and "What was the history that led to this moment?" You'll need to imagine the scene as the words first came to life.

Tone

Tone is what the author feels about the subject and is aligned with attitude. "Tone is conveyed through diction (choice and use of words and phrases), viewpoint, syntax (grammar; how you put words and phrases together), and level of formality."[1]

Tempo

Tempo refers to the pace of the words. Punctuation refers to variation in tempo as well as selective vocal emphasis on specific words or phrases.

The tendency of most reciters is to race through a passage, speeding through to get to the end before it leaks out of their brains. Fight this tendency. Slow down. It takes time for the words that you speak to be absorbed by the people listening. If you go too fast, you're doing everybody a disservice.

In practice, exaggerate a slow pace. A reasonable benchmark is a hundred words per minute. Take breaks. Most speakers don't use silence well. Let your words do the work. If you do, then the other parts of your delivery, such as making eye contact with the audience, will come naturally enough.

Inflection

We don't speak all words evenly. Inflection is the adjustment of volume and pitch when speaking. This is the natural way that we speak. Why so much concern about presenting the recitation in one's natural voice and manner? Because of the honesty it conveys. It can stand on its own. The Word of God doesn't need your voice to warble or your arms to wave, it just needs to be spoken in a way that people understand. So, put away the grandiose gestures and melodramatic mannerisms. They just don't seem honest.

I was attracted to the gospel, to the faith, because, in the midst of beautiful Biblical passages that were full of hope and a higher

---

[1] 155 Words to Describe an Author's Tone

calling, there were thieves, deceivers, and adulterers—and those were the good guys! Somehow, contained in all that messiness, was the message's purity. The gospel is a message for the sick, not for the perfect. There is no pretentiousness when the heroes are murderers, tramps, and backstabbers! That's why a reciter, in order to be faithful to our faith, should deliver the recitation with an honest and sincere expression of the message. In our natural conversation, there's an ebb and flow of intensity and pace. You shouldn't maintain a breakneck velocity and roaring volume for an entire recitation. On the other hand, you don't want to be too soft and plodding. There needs to be a rhythm to your intensity, a rise and fall such as occurs in many songs.

What Do I Do with My Hands?

If this is your question, then it means that you don't yet "own" the words. The passage is still external to you. You are still trying to "act" like someone. It's only when you own the passage, when the words become part of your breath, that your body will become naturally involved in the communication.

We all use our bodies in normal conversation, some more than others, but all of us do it. So instead of diverting too much energy trying to control each body part, it's better to know the passage so well that you just use your body as you normally would to convey the meaning of your recitation. Your hands and every other expressive part of your body will help you to communicate.

There are some general guidelines. Keep your elbows away from your body and make your motions smooth, not abrupt. Smooth is important because it takes even longer for the audience to understand and to absorb motions than it does to absorb words.

Keep your hands out of your pockets and don't cross your arms—at least not for extended periods of time

Thomas L. Griffin

MY RECITATION STORY: COLIN EARLE

Colin Earle

I always considered memorization to be a relatively private thing and didn't really want to share in front of the whole body. It was probably encouragement from a couple of friends that brought me to realize that it could be a benefit and an encouragement to the body. I'm still always nervous and even still a little hesitant to do it. I never want to be a show-off, and I have a hard time receiving praise from others. I want them to praise God and be blessed by His word being spoken.

I've done a handful of recitations and have gained an appreciation for presenting God's word and not just reciting it—but using all the gifts that He has given me to really showcase the word. One of the things that really blessed me was reciting passages that were monologues or had some dialogue in them. I could put myself in the speaker's voice and feel the force of the words from the exhortation of Moses in Deuteronomy 30 to the vitriol of the crowds in Luke 23 to the boldness of Stephen in Acts 7.

Another blessing of reciting large passages of scripture was the transformation of otherwise "wasted time." I would memorize during commutes or memorize during long runs while I was training for marathons. Instead of grousing about the commute or wanting to quit on a run, I would get fully absorbed in a passage of Scripture. That might seem like a small thing, but the Lord was certainly doing a work on my heart, and He redeemed that time.

9

Recitation Art

Art provides another dimension to recitation. Up to this point, we have discussed tone, tempo, inflection, and body language, and how these all add layers to deepen the message. Build on this synergy by including art. The message becomes greater than the sum of its parts, so rich with meaning that it's vast. Art creates a visual connection to the audio message. This, in turn, lays a foundation for memory.

Selecting art isn't just about finding something pretty to be a backdrop. It is finding the visual representation of the verbal message. Find a painting that speaks forgiveness, a sculpture that depicts struggle, a quilt that shows anger, or a carving that casts confusion. Find art that fits the passage, and it will help your audience to remember the message. Art should support and reinforce the spoken word.

Some art was created specifically to depict a portion of the Bible, but much art is secular. If using secular art to support Scripture recitation, you may be building a bridge to the lost.

As you prepare to recite, look for some art that speaks to you, as well as a meaning that connects it with your passage. Paintings, sculptures, and photography are all good options. It's best if the art is not so startling as to be distracting but be clear about your intention.

The following are examples of art used in previous recitations.

Thomas L. Griffin

Reconciliation

by Josefina de Vasconcellos

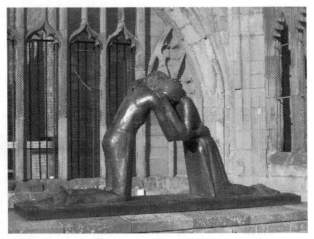

Reconciliation by Josefina de Vasconcellos

Related to 2 Corinthians 5:17–19 ESV

Therefore, if anyone is in Christ, he is a new creation. The old has passed away; behold, the new has come. All this is from God, who through Christ reconciled us to himself and gave us the ministry of reconciliation; that is, in Christ God was reconciling the world to himself, not counting their trespasses against them, and entrusting to us the message of reconciliation.

This incredible sculpture reinforces the words of the passage. The two people seem to melt into each other, and there's a sense of sorrow and relief. The embrace is heartfelt and helps me to understand the meaning of being reconciled to God.

Road with Cypress and Star

By Vincent Van Gogh

Vincent Van Gogh, Kröller-Müller Museum

Related to Genesis 22:1–18 NIV

Some time later God tested Abraham. ... Then God said, "Take your son, your only son, whom you love—Isaac—and go to the region of Moriah. Sacrifice him there as a burnt offering on a mountain I will show you." ... Abraham answered, "God himself will provide the lamb for the burnt offering, my son." And the two of them went on together ... Then he reached out his hand and took the knife to slay his son. But the angel of the *Lord* called out to him from heaven, "Abraham!

Abraham!" "Here I am," he replied. "Do not lay a hand on the boy," he said. "Do not do anything to him. Now I know that you fear God, because you have not withheld from me your son, your only son." Abraham looked up and there in a thicket he saw a ram caught by its horns. ... I will surely bless you and make your descendants as numerous as the stars in the sky and as the sand on the seashore. ... *T*hrough your offspring all nations on earth will be blessed, because you have obeyed me."

Connection

Road with Cypress and Star confronts us with a paradox. From the horizontal middle of the painting, your eye either travels down to the common elements of mundane life, or your eye rises above to stars bursting with color. The cypress tree seems to connect heaven and earth, and the wheat-colored grass or shrubs for the boundary line.

For Abraham, the sky represents the promise of Genesis 22:17–18 NIV, "descendants as numerous as the stars in the sky" and all nations on earth being blessed through his offspring. And yet the dirt road he was traveling was all he could see, that is, until he looked up.

Elijah on a hill

By Kathryn T. Maxwell

Elijah on a hill by Kathryn T. Maxwell

Related to 1 Kings 19:9–13 ESV

There he came to a cave and lodged in it. And behold, the word of the *Lord* came to him, and he said to him, "What are you doing here, Elijah?" He said, "I have been very jealous for the *Lord*, the God of hosts. For the people of Israel have forsaken your covenant, thrown down your altars, and killed your prophets with the sword, and I, even I only, am left, and they seek my life, to take it away." And he said, "Go out and stand on the mount before the *Lord*." And behold, the *Lord* passed by, and a great and strong wind tore the mountains and broke in pieces the rocks before the *Lord*, but the *Lord* was not in the wind. And after the wind an earthquake, but the *Lord* was not in the earthquake. And after the earthquake a fire, but the *Lord* was not in the fire. And after the fire the sound of a low whisper.

And when Elijah heard it, he wrapped his face in
his cloak and went out and stood at the entrance of
the cave. And behold, there came a voice to him and
said, "What are you doing here, Elijah?"

Connection

Elijah seems so alone in this painting, contemplating something
and feeling a bit sorry for himself. The feel is of a desert—a barren
landscape, hard and cold. His posture, feet wide, arms forward,
indicates that he's looking for something but not knowing where.
Searching into the distance with his eyes. It's a beautiful painting
that matches the Lord's question of him: "What are you doing here,
Elijah?"

Mandala of the Seed

by Jyoti Shai Art Ashram

Cosmic Seed by Jyoti Shai Art Ashram

Related to Titus 3:3–7 ESV

For we ourselves were once foolish, disobedient, led astray, slaves to various passions and pleasures, passing our days in malice and envy, hated by others and hating one another. But when the goodness and loving kindness of God our Savior appeared, he saved us, not because of works done by us in righteousness, but according to his own mercy, by the washing of regeneration and renewal of the Holy Spirit, whom he poured out on us richly through Jesus Christ our Savior, so that being justified by his grace we might become heirs according to the hope of eternal life.

Connection

Hidden in the story of the birth and childhood of Jesus is an understanding of the Cross. The seed has to die in order that the new life, which is the rebirth of the soul, can take place. The word of God is present in the cave of the heart, as a seed of life, which is planted in every human being.

This passage was recited by a man who had returned to the Lord and this passage was read at his baptism. Now, a few years after his baptism, he wanted to memorize and recite the passage. For him, this passage reminds him of his rebirth, and the art is of a seed brought to life in a dazzlingly beautiful world.

The Trinity

by Andrei Rublev (Tretyakov Gallery, Moscow)

The Trinity by Andrei Rublev

Related to Genesis 18 NIV

The icon (The Hospitality of Abraham). Abraham "was sitting at the entrance to his tent in the heat of the day" by the Oak of Mamre and saw three men standing in front of him, who in the next chapter were revealed as angels, who represented the Christian Trinity, "one God in three persons"—the Father, the Son (Jesus Christ), and the Holy Spirit. The angels were depicted as talking, not eating. The silent communion of the three angels is the center of the composition.

The center of the composition is the cup with the calf's head. It hints at the crucifixion sacrifice and serves as the reminder of the Eucharist (the left and the right angels' figures make a silhouette that resembles a cup).

The left angel symbolizes God the Father. He blesses the cup, yet his hand is painted in a distance, as if he passes the cup to the central angel. The central angel represents Jesus Christ, who in turn blesses the cup as well and accepts it with a bow, as if saying, "My Father, if it is possible, may this cup be taken from me. Yet not as I will, but as you will" (Matthew 26:39 NIV).

The Oak of Mamre can be interpreted as the tree of life, and it serves as a reminder of the Jesus's death on the cross and his subsequent resurrection, which opened the way to eternal life. The Trinity expresses unity and love between all things: "That they may all be one, just as you, Father, are in me, and I in you, that they also may be in us, so that the world may believe that you have sent me" (John 17:21 ESV).

The Rescue of David

by Danielle Harth

2 Samuel 22 (The Rescue of David) by Danielle Harth

Related to Deuteronomy 30:11–20 NIV

Now what I am commanding you today is not too difficult for you or beyond your reach. It is not up in heaven, so that you have to ask, "Who will ascend into heaven to get it and proclaim it to us so we may obey it?" Nor is it ... 14 No, the word is very near you; it is in your mouth and in your heart so you may obey it. See, I set before you today life and prosperity, death and destruction. For I command you today to love the Lord your God, to walk in obedience to him, and to keep his commands, decrees and laws; then you will live and increase, and the Lord your God will bless you in the land you are entering to possess ... This day I call the heavens and the earth as witnesses against you that I have set before you life and death, blessings and curses. Now choose life, so that you and your children may live and that you may love the Lord your God, listen to his voice, and hold fast to him. For the Lord is your life, and he will give you many years in the land he swore to give to your fathers, Abraham, Isaac and Jacob.

Connection

The stark contrast in the painting between fire and water matches the choice that Moses is presenting in his message to the Israelites—life and death, blessings and curses. Make your choice between these powerful forces. In the painting, there appears to be a third element, mediating and separating the choices, standing in the gap.

10

Onstage Techniques

Locating the Characters Onstage

As you begin to rehearse onstage, determine the characters in the passage and assign them a place in the room. When you refer to each character, then you'll look in the direction of where you located each one. This can provide an important clarification for the audience during the recitation and can also serve as a memory prompt for the reciter.

Example 1

In a recitation of Luke 5:17–26 NIV (Jesus forgives and heals a paralyzed man), the characters were positioned as follows:

- Pharisees were located downstage right.
- Jesus was midcenter stage.
- The friends who carried the paralyzed man were upstage left.
- The paralyzed man appears later, downstage left.

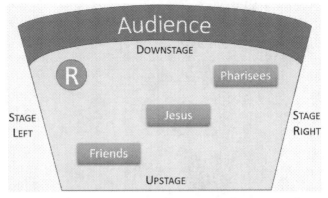

*One day Jesus was teaching, and Pharisees and
teachers of the law were sitting there.*

(glances downstage right)

*They had come from every village of Galilee
and from Judea and Jerusalem.*

(looks center)

And the power of the Lord was with Jesus to heal the sick.

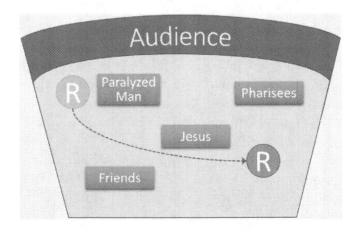

(moves upstage right and looks towards downstage left)

Some men came carrying a paralyzed man on a mat and tried to take him into the house to lay him before Jesus. When they could not find a way to do this because of the crowd, they went up on the roof and lowered him on his mat through the tiles into the middle of the crowd, right in front of Jesus. When Jesus saw their faith, he said, "Friend, your sins are forgiven."

(glances downstage right)

The Pharisees and the teachers of the law began thinking to themselves, "Who is this fellow who speaks blasphemy? Who can forgive sins but God alone?"

(motions to center stage)

Jesus knew what they were thinking and asked

(looks downstage right)

"Why are you thinking these things in your hearts? Which is easier: to say, 'Your sins are forgiven,' or to say, 'Get up and walk'? But I want you to know that the Son of Man has authority on earth to forgive sins."

(looks to the audience)

So he said to the paralyzed man,

(looks downstage left)

"I tell you, get up, take your mat and go home." Immediately he stood up in front of them, took what he had been lying on and went home praising God.

(looks to the center of the audience)

*Everyone was amazed and gave praise to God. They were filled
with awe and said, "We have seen remarkable things today."*

Example 2

A recitation of Colossians 1:13–20 NIV, particularly Colossians
1:19–20 NIV, in the section on the supremacy of Christ.

*For God was pleased to have all **his** fullness dwell in **him**, and
through **him** to reconcile to **himself** all things, whether things on earth
or things in heaven, by making peace through **his** blood, shed on the cross.*

When you read this passage, at least in the NIV, you find an
ambiguity in the personal pronoun references "him," "himself," and
"his." Based on context, it is clear the participants are the Trinity
persons of the Father and Son—but which "his/him" is the Father,
and which is the Son?

In order to clarify, the two personas were located as follows:

- The Father was located at the top left of the back wall.
- The Son was located stage right, near the reciter.

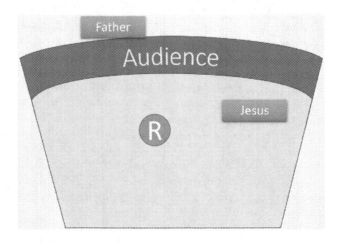

Now, put the passage in the body of a reciter, one who understands the principle of locating the people onstage, and you will find body language that locates the bold text as the Father, and the nonitalicized text as the Son:

> *For God was pleased to have all*
> **(gestures to top left)** his *fullness dwell in*
> **(gestures with right hand)** him, *and through*
> **(gestures with right hand)** him *to reconcile to*
> **(gestures to top left)** himself *all things, whether things*
> *on earth or things in heaven, by making peace through*
> **(gestures with right hand)** his *blood, shed on the cross.*

Eye Contact

Audiences want to feel a connection with the speaker, and the only way to connect with someone is to look that person in the eye.

Eye contact is one of the most important elements of delivery. There is no trick to make this easy. If you look at the wall or the aisle or the post, we all will be able to tell. Your delivery will appear aloof and distant to your audience. It's hard, and you may need to learn to stomach the butterflies and get over it. Look your audience in the eyes.

If you're talking to a large group of people, look at that group of people. Bring everyone in. The people in the back row should feel as engaged and respected by you as people right in the front row.

Recall that the goal is to communicate naturally, and that can't be done without looking into their eyes. Imagine a conversation in which the person with whom you're conversing always looks away from you and never at you. That would be awkward. An audience is the same, except it may not be possible to look each person in the eye. It's enough to connect with a few. It lets everyone know that you're "with us" and not aloof or distant. You need to dwell with your audience.

As you rehearse, determine when the appropriate time will

be to move your focus onto another person. By doing this, you're adding "formatting." In a written document, there's punctuation, paragraphs, and headings to guide the reader. In a presentation, the presenter adds the formatting through the way he or she delivers the message. The movement of your eyes is one way to add formatting.

Looking away from your audience once in a while during a presentation isn't negative. You don't have to look at your audience for 100 percent of your presentation. Instead of forcing your eyes to remain on your audience, realize that it's okay to look down, to the side, or off in the distance for brief moments.

In any case, practice your eye movement. There's no need to wait for the recitation to invent your movement. You can plan it and practice it so that your eye movement is included in your rehearsal. This can also be a memory trigger for you (see the section on memorization techniques).

Don't Be a Sprinkler or a Tennis Umpire

A sprinkler presenter goes systematically across the room. A tennis umpire presenter looks first to the left, then to the right, back and forth. After a few rounds it can be predictable and distracting.

Breathing

Within the passage that you will be reciting, you will need to find the rhythm, based on variations in volume and cadence, and that involves breathing. Sometimes, the word being spoken is meant to come as you inhale the next breath. This happens at a starting conjunction. As you study the Bible with a mind to speaking it, you will find that there are cases in which the conjunction is at the start of a phrase, and this conjunction needs special consideration. It contributes a certain camaraderie and closeness between the speaker and the audience. You find them primarily when a passage is quoting somebody speaking, because this is an element that's natural in speech.

The Pickup Note

Be on the lookout for words that act as transitions or starters. These grace words, or "pickup notes," are words added as breaths. They are the spoken equivalent of artistic white space. Consider the passage from Ecclesiastes 9:15 NIV: "Now there lived in that city a man poor but wise, and he saved the city by his wisdom." And notice that the word *now* is not spoken forcefully or evenly but is brushed past, on the way to "there lived." When you start reading the Bible like this, hearing the breaths, it sounds more familiar and less clinical.

Here's a similar example. How do you read the first word *now* of Deuteronomy 30:11 NIV? "Now what I am commanding you today is not too difficult for you or beyond your reach."

Is it an emphatic "*Now*"? Or is it softer? In this case, I feel that the "now" acts like a pickup note in music. It's a bridge between the previous phrase and the one that's coming. The pickup note is voiced softer and abbreviated.

"Now what I am commanding you today is not too difficult for you or beyond your reach."

The musical term "pickup note" refers to an

Pickup Note
A note that occurs before the first full measure of a musical composition

<no caption>

unstressed *pickup* or lead-in *note* or group of *notes* that precedes the first accented *note* of a phrase. It's used quite often in songs where words need to make sense and fit into the rhythm.

There are other words used as starting conjunctions, or "pickup notes:"

See

> *See, I set before you today life and prosperity, death and destruction.* (Deuteronomy 30:11 NIV)

Now

> *Now no shrub had yet appeared on the earth and no plant had yet sprung up, for ...* (Genesis 2:5 NIV)

> *Now Lot, who was moving about with Abram, also had flocks and herds and tents.* (Genesis 13:5 NIV)

> *Now the men had said to her, "This oath you made us swear will not be ...* (Joshua 2:17 NIV)

> *Now he who supplies seed to the sower and bread for food ...* (2 Corinthians 9:10 NIV)

For

> *For I see that you are full of bitterness and captive to sin."* (Acts 8:23 NIV)

> *For if someone with a weak conscience sees you, with all your knowledge ...* (1 Corinthians 8:10 NIV)

For *I do not want to see you now and make only a passing visit* ... (1 Corinthians 16:7 NIV)

Not all starting conjunctions act as pickup notes. For example, the "but" in this passage:

> **But** *the land could not support them while they stayed together, for their possessions were so great that they were not able to stay together.* (Genesis 13:6 NIV)

The "but" is important to the meaning of the sentence and needs full voice. It is not a pickup note. Or if the word is combined with another word, as in "Now then" or "See to it" in these verses.

> *"**Now then**, please swear to me by the Lord that you will show kindness* ... (Joshua 2:12 NIV)

> **See to it** *that no one falls short of the grace of God and that no bitter root* ... (Hebrews 12:15 NIV)

The starting conjunction combined with a few other words is conveying an important meaning to the passage. In Revelation 5:5 NIV, the "see" is definitely not a pickup note.

> **See**, *the Lion of the tribe of Judah, the Root of David, has triumphed.*

It is an emphatic "**see**," forcefully instructing the reader to consider what the lion of the tribe of Judah has accomplished. The "see" in this passage from Numbers is more of an even direction to investigate.

> **See** *what the land is like and whether the people who live there are strong or weak, few or many.* (Numbers 13:18 NIV)

> **See** *how the faithful city has become a prostitute! She once was full of justice; righteousness used to dwell in her—but now murderers!* (Isaiah 1:21 NIV)

In these cases, the "see" functions as an imperative verb. Imperative verbs don't leave room for questions or discussion, even if the sentence has a polite tone. And they are definitely not pickup notes!

11

The Day of the Recitation

After so much preparation, the day of your recitation will arrive. There will be a flurry of activity, and you'll want to keep your focus. Make sure that someone who will protect you from the myriad distractions that may arise is with you.

Right up to the moment you're reciting, people may ask you to move things onstage, read an announcement, convey information to someone onstage, or other seemingly innocuous requests. I suggest that you should either politely decline or delegate the task to your assistant. You need to keep your focus, and these things can complicate your thoughts and become obstacles to your success.

Checklist

When the day of the recitation arrives, it's important for you to stay focused on the message. The coordinator will need to take charge to ensure that all of the details are taken care of.

Checklist for Reciters	Checklist for Leaders
✓ Arrive at the venue 30 minutes before the service begins.	✓ Graphics have been provided to the projection team.
✓ Microphone positioned (esp. headset) and an onstage sound check has been complete.	✓ Projection team has been briefed on when graphics should be displayed.
✓ The person on book has a copy of the text.	✓ Order of worship and the transition to the recitation has been defined, and all involved people have been notified.
✓ Voice has been warmed.	✓ Video recorder in place.
✓ Performed a dry-run of the passage with the on-book person.	✓ Arrangements have been made to move any onstage obstacles for the reciter.
✓ Appropriately dressed.	

Visuals

There are two graphics we like to include when reciters are onstage. The first is a family picture for before the recitation, and the second is a graphic to display during the recitation.

Family Picture

In addition to the reference slide, we like to communicate something about the reciter—name, family, and profession. It is one way that we grow in fellowship. We display a family picture with the following goals:

- Making connections between people. Someone may know the father, but not realize who his children are. They may know the mother but not know who her husband is. It's not just about the reciter. Seeing the picture helps with making these connections, especially for newcomers.
- Providing the family context in which God's Word is being expressed in life. If I see someone reciting a passage on perseverance, and I see that they have lots of kids, it may make a bridge that connects me to the reciter, or to someone in the reciter's family.

Steve, YouHyung, Benjamin, and Bethany Gibbons

Example of a family introduction slide

Graphic during the Recitation

A graphic or PowerPoint slide that shows the reference of the passage and a backdrop for the passage. We like to incorporate meaningful art in the backdrop. The slide also helps to remind the audience about where the passage can be found, and is a reference for after the recitation, when

Background slide for a recitation

reviewing pictures and videos, so that it is clear which passage is involved.

Clothing

Since we are not acting like anybody other than ourselves, we should dress as we normally would. There are only a few other considerations:

- You will need someplace to put the battery pack for the wireless headset mic.
- Shoes that are compatible with the obstacles and texture of the stage.
- Minimize distracting clothing or accoutrements.

The Distraction

Every reciter has a story about "the distraction." For some it was a friend in the audience, or a child crying, or sudden door slam. Often it is our own mind conjuring up childhood memories or a favorite event—anything that is not the next few words that you're meant to be reciting.

You can prepare for and defend against the distraction.

- Practice with distractions in your environment. Play the radio as you drive to work and recite over the top of that noise.
- Practice by using the start-anywhere technique (see memorization techniques section in this book)
- Practice with the on-book person so that you are in sync.

The Video

A video recording allows people who weren't present for the recitation to be able to experience it, and for those who were present to re-experience it. For the reciter, a video is an excellent technique to *pre*-experience the recitation. Record a video of your recitation and then watch it to identify any mannerisms, motions, phrasing, tempo, or tone that detract from the message. Critically look for anything that would draw the audience's attention away from the message that you're delivering.

Take the time to make a "clean" recording of your recitation that can be posted to a website like https://ByHeart.org. This can serve as a resource for others to use in Bible studies and to augment services or gatherings. Doing this recording before the day of the recitation will give you a big boost in confidence and will serve to identify any problem areas in time for you to make the necessary changes. Recording beforehand also removes the stress and possible distractions of recording the video live, and it allows you to record the video from locations and perspectives that may be prohibitive in a live setting.

12

After the Recitation

Now that you have invested so much in the passage and have a deeper understanding of it, you should recite it at every opportunity. Yes, you have done it at a Sunday service for your church family, and it was a wonderful experience. It will be different and still wonderful to do it again in a different venue. The intent of this chapter is to provide you with ideas for extending and building on your experience.

Repeat the Recitation

Youth Group/Sunday School

If the youth in your church didn't see your recitation, then bring it to them. Their teachers will be grateful, and the kids will enjoy the special attention. The group is smaller, and don't be surprised if this experience feels incredibly intimate and powerful. You will not just be reciting a passage, you will also be making the Bible more personal for the young audience members and modeling the results of devoted study. If you have children of your own, then it will be more important to them that you recited in their youth group or Sunday school class than if you recited at any other venue.

Homeless Shelter

Faith-based shelters for the homeless sometimes include an outreach event. Bring your recitation to them. You don't need to teach or even comment on the passage. It's enough if you simply recite your passage. Any more than that is a bonus for the people who run the shelter. My only warning is that these can be difficult venues because the audience may not be completely encouraging. There will probably be people who are disinterested or actively uninvolved. On the other hand, there will be some people who embrace the message and these people will lift your spirits and exalt our Lord. In either case, whether disinterested or devoted, everyone will benefit. The Word will not go out and return empty.

At Another Church

How better to connect the community of believers than to share the core of what unites us? Ask if you can recite your passage at another church. Since most recitations are only one to two minutes in duration, it isn't a major disruption to the order of worship at the church. It's also a chance to connect the body of believers and possibly inspire others to dig deeper into the Word. Don't be offended if the church is wary of giving the stage to an outsider. It will be easier if you know somebody who belongs to the church and can vouch for you.

Help Someone Else

The principles of discipleship kick in. You have been blessed and have learned. Pass these on to another person. It's in the discipleship covenant that you'll propagate what has been invested in you during the recitation preparation. You may just want to participate in another recitation, but you also may want to join the preparation journey of another reciter, or even initiate an event and lead a recitation.

If you are interested in leading a recitation, please refer to my other book, *The Art of Leading Scripture Reciters.*

Begin Anew

Choose another passage and start afresh. The next time through, there will be new things to learn, not only about the passage but also about the process.

Choose someone to disciple you through the process. Resist the temptation to do it "on your own" or to be overconfident. It will always be a big deal to recite, and if you casually walk through the process, it won't have the impact on your life that it should.

Appendix—Categories of Passages

The following groups can help in selecting passages:

- Story (Narratives)
  o Acts of Faith
  o Prophecy
- Teaching
  o Admonishment & Worldly Influence
  o The Christian Walk
- Praise
  o God's Love for Us
  o Person and Deity of Christ
  o Praise

The Scriptures below are arranged in these groups. A representative excerpt from the cited passage follows each citation.

Story (Narratives)

Acts of Faith

- Hebrews 11:8–16 NIV: "By faith he made his home in the promised land like a stranger in a foreign country."

- Acts 7:2–53 NIV: "The patriarchs were jealous of Joseph, they sold him as a slave into Egypt. But God was with him."
- Acts 8:26–35 NIV: "So he started out, and on his way he met an Ethiopian eunuch, an important official."
- 1 Kings 18:22–40 NIV: "Choose one of the bulls and prepare it first, since there are so many of you. Call on the name of your god, but do not light the fire."
- 1 Kings 19:9–13 NIV": "Then a great and powerful wind tore the mountains apart and shattered the rocks before the Lord, but the Lord was not in the wind. After the wind there was an earthquake."
- Esther 4:1–17 NIV: "And who knows but that you have come to your royal position for such a time as this?"
- Acts 5:29–39 NIV: "But a Pharisee named Gamaliel, a teacher of the law, who was honored by all the people, stood up in the Sanhedrin."

Prophecy

- Isaiah 53:1–12 NIV: "He took up our pain and bore our suffering, yet we considered him punished by God, stricken by him, and afflicted. But he was pierced for our transgressions."
- Psalm 110:1–7 KJV: "The Lord said unto my Lord, Sit thou at my right hand, until I make thine enemies thy footstool."
- Isaiah 6:1–13 NIV: "The temple was filled with smoke. 'Woe to me!' I cried. 'I am ruined! For I am a man of unclean lips, and I live among a people of unclean lips, and my eyes have seen the King, the Lord Almighty.'"
- Hebrews 7:13–8:13 NIV: "But he became a priest with an oath when God said to him: 'The Lord has sworn and will not change his mind: "You are a priest forever."' Because

of this oath, Jesus has become the guarantor of a better covenant."

- 1 Kings 18:41–46 NIV: "The seventh time the servant reported, 'A cloud as small as a man's hand is rising from the sea.' So Elijah said, 'Go and tell Ahab, "Hitch up your chariot and go down before the rain stops you."'"
- 2 Kings 6:8–19 NIV: "'Don't be afraid,' the prophet answered. 'Those who are with us are more than those who are with them.' And Elisha prayed, 'Open his eyes, Lord, so that he may see.'"
- Luke 1:39–50 NIV: "And Mary said: 'My soul glorifies the Lord and my spirit rejoices in God my Savior, for he has been mindful of the humble state of his servant. From now on all generations will call me blessed.'"
- Isaiah 9:1–7 NIV: "By the Way of the Sea, beyond the Jordan—the people walking in darkness have seen a great light; on those living in the land of deep darkness a light has dawned."
- Isaiah 53:2–8 NIV: "He was despised and rejected by mankind, a man of suffering, and familiar with pain. Like one from whom people hide their faces he was despised, and we held him in low esteem."

Teaching

Admonishment & Worldly Influence

- Ecclesiastes 1:2–2:26 NIV: "I have seen all the things that are done under the sun; all of them are meaningless, a chasing after the wind."
- 1 Timothy 1:1–20 NIV: "They want to be teachers of the law, but they do not know what they are talking about or what they so confidently affirm."

- 1 Corinthians 11:17–23 NIV: "As a result, one person remains hungry and another gets drunk. Don't you have homes to eat and drink in?"
- James 2:14–26 ESV: "And one of you says to them, 'Go in peace, be warmed and filled,' without giving them the things needed for the body, what good is that?"
- James 4:1–6 NLT: "Yet you don't have what you want because you don't ask God for it. And even when you ask, you don't get it because your motives are all wrong."
- James 2:1–26 NIV: "Suppose a man comes into your meeting wearing a gold ring and fine clothes, and a poor man in filthy old clothes also comes in."
- Acts 20:28–32 NIV: "I know that after I leave, savage wolves will come in among you and will not spare the flock."
- Romans 6:1–14 NIV: "Shall we go on sinning so that grace may increase?"
- Isaiah 1:11–12 NIV: "'The multitude of your sacrifices—what are they to me?' says the Lord. 'I have more than enough of burnt offerings.'"
- Romans 3:10–17 NIV: "All have turned away, they have together become worthless; there is no one who does good, not even one."

The Christian Walk

- James 1:26–27 NIV: "Religion that God our Father accepts as pure and faultless is this: to look after orphans and widows."
- 1 Peter 3:15–16 NIV: "Be prepared to give an answer to everyone who asks you to give the reason for the hope that you have."
- James 1:2–18 NIV: "Consider it pure joy, my brothers and sisters, whenever you face trials of many kinds."

- James 1:19–27 NIV: "Do not merely listen to the word, and so deceive yourselves. Do what it says."
- James 4:7–12 NLT: "Humble yourselves before the Lord, and he will lift you up in honor."
- 1Peter 1:1–25 NIV: "Though you have not seen him, you love him; and even though you do not see him now, you believe in him and are filled with an inexpressible and glorious joy."
- Romans 8:1–4 NIV: "And so he condemned sin in the flesh, in order that the righteous requirement of the law might be fully met in us."
- Joshua 1:1–9 NIV: "Be strong and courageous, because you will lead these people to inherit the land I swore to their ancestors to give them."
- Hebrews 12:1–2 NIV: "Therefore, since we are surrounded by such a great cloud of witnesses."
- Romans 8:12–15 NIV: "The Spirit you received does not make you slaves, so that you live in fear again; rather."
- Romans 8:1–11 NIV: "Therefore, there is now no condemnation for those who are in Christ Jesus, because through Christ Jesus the law of the Spirit who gives life."
- 1 Corinthians 9:19–23 NIV: "To the Jews I became like a Jew, to win the Jews. To those under the law I became like one under the law."

Praise

God's Love for Us

- Psalm 139:1–24 NIV: "You have searched me, Lord, and you know me. You know when I sit and when I rise."
- Ephesians 3:14–21 NIV: "Being rooted and established in love, may have power, together with all the Lord's holy

people, to grasp how wide and long and high and deep is the love of Christ."

- Jeremiah 29:11–13 NIV: "For I know the plans I have for you," declares the Lord."
- 1 Corinthians 15:55–57 NIV: "The sting of death is sin, and the power of sin is the law."
- Titus 3:3–7 NIV: "He saved us, not because of righteous things we had done, but because of his mercy."
- Psalm 121:1–8 NIV: "I lift up my eyes to the mountains— where does my help come from? My help comes from the Lord."
- Isaiah 43:1–7 NIV: "When you pass through the waters, I will be with you; and when you pass through the rivers."
- Ephesians 2:4–10 NIV: "For it is by grace you have been saved, through faith—and this is not from yourselves, it is the gift of God."
- John 3:16–21 NIV: "Whoever believes in him is not condemned, but whoever does not believe stands condemned already because they have not believed."
- Psalm 51:1–12 NIV: "For I know my transgressions, and my sin is always before me. Against you, you only, have I sinned."
- Isaiah 55:1–9 NIV: "Come, all you who are thirsty, come to the waters; and you who have no money, come, buy and eat! Come, buy wine and milk without money and without cost."
- Titus 3:3–7 NIV: "At one time we too were foolish, disobedient, deceived and enslaved by all kinds of passions and pleasures. We lived in malice and envy, being hated and hating one another."

- Colossians 1:13–20 NIV: "The Son is the image of the invisible God, the firstborn over all creation. For in him all things were created: things in heaven and on earth, visible and invisible."
- John 1:1–18 NIV: "In him was life, and that life was the light of all mankind. The light shines in the darkness, and the darkness has not overcome it."
- Hebrews 1:1–6 NIV: "But in these last days he has spoken to us by his Son, whom he appointed heir of all things, and through whom also he made the universe."
- Luke 2:1–12 NLT: "He took with him Mary, to whom he was engaged, who was now expecting a child. And while they were there, the time came for her baby to be born."
- Luke 1:26–38 NIV: Said to her, "Do not be afraid, Mary; you have found favor with God. You will conceive and give birth to a son."
- Luke 2:8–14 NIV: "But the angel said to them, "Do not be afraid. I bring you good news that will cause great joy for all the people."
- Matthew 2:1–12 NIV: "When he had called together all the people's chief priests and teachers of the law, he asked them where the Messiah was to be born."
- Luke 2:1–7 NIV: "So Joseph also went up from the town of Nazareth in Galilee to Judea, to Bethlehem the town of David, because he belonged to the house and line of David."
- Mark 14:1–11 NIV: "She broke the jar and poured the perfume on his head. Some of those present were saying indignantly to one another, 'Why this waste of perfume?'"
- Mark 14:53–65 NIV: "They took Jesus to the high priest, and all the chief priests, the elders and the teachers of the law came together. Peter followed him at a distance, right into the courtyard of the high priest."

- Mark 14:66–72 NIV: "When she saw Peter warming himself, she looked closely at him. "You also were with that Nazarene, Jesus," she said. But he denied it."
- Mark 15:21–37 NIV: "On his way in from the country, and they forced him to carry the cross. They brought Jesus to the place called Golgotha (which means 'the place of the skull')."
- Mark 15: 9–20 NIV: "'What shall I do, then, with the one you call the king of the Jews?' Pilate asked them. 'Crucify him!' they shouted. 'Why? What crime has he committed?' asked Pilate."
- John 1:1–4 NIV: "In the beginning was the Word, and the Word was with God, and the Word was God. He was with God in the beginning."
- Ephesians 1:15–23 KJV: "Far above all principality, and power, and might, and dominion, and every name that is named, not only in this world."
- Luke 5:17–26 NIV: "And tried to take him into the house to lay him before Jesus. When they could not find a way to do this because of the crowd, they went up on the roof and lowered him on his mat."

Praise

- Psalm 19:7–11 NIV: "The law of the Lord is perfect, refreshing the soul. The statutes of the Lord are trustworthy, making wise the simple. The precepts of the Lord are right, giving joy to the heart."
- Psalm 9:7–8 NIV: "The Lord reigns forever; he has established his throne for judgment. He rules the world in righteousness and judges the peoples with equity."

- Psalm 118 NIV: "Give thanks to the Lord, for he is good; his love endures forever. Let Israel say: 'His love endures forever.' Let the house of Aaron say: 'His love endures forever.'"
- Psalm 27:4–5 NIV: "One thing I ask from the Lord, this only do I seek: that I may dwell in the house of the Lord all the days of my life."
- Psalm 18:30–33 NIV: "It is God who arms me with strength and keeps my way secure. He makes my feet like the feet of a deer; he causes me to stand on the heights."

Acknowledgements

With heartfelt gratitude I'd like to thank the following for their contributions and inspiration in supporting and encouraging me in creating this book. To Carol Griffin for being my sounding board, to Carsten Lotz for his unbridled enthusiasm, to Gary Darnell whose keen insight shaped the bulk of the chapter on Biblical interpretation, to Naomi Woodford for her precise editing and valuable suggestions, to Jimmy Martin for his staunch promotion of recitation, to Tom Asai for his steadfast loyalty and inspiring stories of sharing the Gospel, to the Wynn family for their big hearts and great talent, and to Linda Moore for her bravery and enthusiasm.

And to the many people who have boldly spoken the word of truth, including: Linda, Philip D., Jay, Ellie J., Paul, Anna, Rachel, Jim, Ed, Grace, Brad, Tim P., Jake, Jordan, Nathaniel, Annie, Rebecca G., Allison, Abigail, Hannah, Spencer, Casey, Nathaniel, Colin, Carly, Matty O., Dawn, Ben, Wenyu, Mario, Katherine, Jeff N. (both of them!), Galen, Dan & Kyle, Mark & Bradley, Jen & Andrew, Deborah & Nicole, Carol G., Rebecca T., Tom A., Tom S., Robby, Connie, Gary S., Arturo, Nate, Edmund, Tania, Steve C., Mike L., Jay, Jae, Mark W-M, Mike V., Becky C., Philipp L., Käthe, Carsten, Peter, Benjamin, Rebecca E., Kerry, Titus, Frank-Detlef, Lydia, Darren, Rosana, Aleth, Thomas L., Dan G., Igor, Charity, Aghiad, Esli, Felix, Ellie C., Lottie, Ryan, Steve G., Mishal, Jeremy S., Mairi, Gary D., Eric H., Kelly K., Jim Cap., Natalie L., Kori, Imelda, Sujan, Sidney, Julian W., Jeanette, Jamari, Beth W.,

Michael, Natalie P., Lucille (there could only be one!), Regina, David F., Timothy K., Naomi W., Naomi B., Vishal, Nicolas, Verena, Iris, Stefan L., Charity, Raoul, Mike Mc., Abigail B., Kyla S., Ellie H., Sam P., Paige, Caleb (the youngest!), Chris G., Trevor, ...and the one that I can't remember.

About the Author

A software consultant with over a decade of teaching high school physics in his past, Tom grew up in San Leandro, California, where he found the love of his life, Carol. He started reciting Scripture in 1997 and has led hundreds of people through the process of preparing to recite. He has worked with individuals, small teams and large groups, developing the craft of recitations extending from single passages to complex multi-lingual compositions. Blessed with two incredible daughters and the best friends one could imagine, Tom now lives in Frankfurt, Germany where he practices as a consultant and coordinates recitations at the International Christian Fellowship.

Printed in the United States
by Baker & Taylor Publisher Services